We work with clients ɨ varied set of projects, hear from them, in their own words...

"I can remember Hugh's first visit like yesterday. Hugh, I still owe you a lunch :) Teaming up with Hugh and Maize Quest has impacted everything I do in a very positive way. Ag entertainment is taking my business to a level I never thought possible."

—MIKE M., MA

"Thank you for your site visit last spring. It is incredibly helpful to have another set of eyes on our operation and receive insight and recommendations from someone that understands what we do! We would never be charging (and receiving) some of the prices we charge without your suggestions (pushing, shaming)! We are looking forward to working with you again!"

—BILL D., OH

"We would be lost without those Maize Quest Hayride Audio boxes. Whenever they aren't playing music it feels like deadsville out there."

—HANK K., NY

"If we hadn't signed up for your Sunflower Mastermind Group, we'd have had a ****ing disaster."

—KEVIN H., IL

"As the Education & Operations Manager for the North American Farmers' Direct Marketing Association, I am responsible for vetting and selecting speakers for the Educational Program at our organization's annual conference. Hugh McPherson ranks at the top of my list due to his subject knowledge on production, marketing, staffing and event management. His sessions are always full, his personality is engaging, and his ability to educate and inspire our attendees always garners outstanding reviews on our post-event surveys. I would highly recommend Hugh McPherson as a session presenter, as he has always created an exceptional experience for our attendees."

—JEFF WINSTON, NAFDMA

SAVE over $5,420.13 AND 363 Hours.

The GIANT *"Get More Customers To Your Business Book Buyer's Bonus Package"* is at:
www.hughMcPherson.com/MoreCustomers

As much as I would like to include everything possible in this book, it is IMPOSSIBLE. Plus, some people learn better from hearing, seeing videos, working in groups, or doing worksheets.

So, I'm including TONS of extras, bonuses and savings as a "Thank You" for taking the first step in growing your business using the tactics in the book.
You'll find:

✔ Hugh's Recommended Tools – An ever-growing list of over 27 software and hardware options to help you implement what you learn in this book (363 Hours VALUE)

✔ Goal Without A Plan is a Wish Workshop ($697 VALUE)

✔ The Cross-Marketing Multiplier Presentation ($697 VALUE)

✔ Event Tsunami Strategic Event Marketing Program (30% OFF)

✔ Views to Visitors Click-By-Click Facebook Marketing Program (30% OFF)

✔ Social Advertising: DECODED FREE Video Presentation on Facebook Lead Ads, plus complete online course (30% OFF)

✔ Agritourism Manager Boot Camp – The #1 Agritourism Employee Management System (30% OFF)

✔ Seasonal Manager Boot Camp – A Complete Employee Management System for ANY Seasonal Business (30% OFF)

- ✓ Platinum Set-up Package from TicketSpice.com for our clients and friends ONLY – ($700 VALUE)
- ✓ Sunflower Festival FREE 3-Video Series, PLUS Sunflower Mastermind Group Registration ($200 OFF)
- ✓ *"Your Event Pricing Is Too Low And I Can Prove It"* Profitable pricing video Presentation ($497 VALUE)
- ✓ *"Adventures In Delegating"* 5-Part Video Series to make you an effective task delegator and free up your time ($497 VALUE)

YES! We've done ALL this stuff first-hand running our farm, pick-your-own fruit orchards, corn maze, fun park, birthday party center, sunflower festival, and winery.

YES! All this is really available to you, included.

YES! You can't do everything in this book in a single day, week, month or even year.

YES! You can reference what you need and get back to work QUICKLY, so keep this book handy.

YES! We offer plenty of ways to get MORE detailed information particularly through our popular online courses.

YES! You CAN do this! This book is FULL of positive energy to power you through each SHORT, DOABLE action step.

YES! We are REAL people and you can call me at the farm at 717-382-4878 ext. 102 to discuss ANY of our programs - *Hugh*

The GIANT *"Get More Customers To Your Business Book Buyer's Bonus Package"* is at:
www.HughMcPherson.com/MoreCustomers

Customers Coming Out of Your Ears

Hugh McPherson

TABLE OF CONTENTS

INTRODUCTION

Depression-era grandparents: "Waste not want not." "You don't work, you don't eat." "Penny saved is a penny earned." "Clean your plate."

All of these sayings might sound familiar if you grew up like I did, with Depression Era parents or grandparents. Mabel McPherson – my paternal grandmother, whom we referred to somewhat formally as "Grandmother" – was a babysitter, farm bookkeeper, and role model along with her spinster sister Ethelind "Lindy" Anderson.

Grandmother and Aunt Lindy ran a tight ship, the way they had been taught as children, and the way the Great Depression had mandated for survival. Their house was our go-to place when Mom and Dad had an American Agri-women conference, a National Peach Council convention, fire company meeting, or other adventure that wouldn't be entertaining enough for me and my two sisters, Gretchen and Sarah, to tag along.

Those two ladies, along with Al and Evelyn Spory on the maternal side, modeled the efficient, modest, borderline austere lifestyle. Nothing was wasted.

Oh, how the modern world has strayed. One could lament the culture of disposable pleasures at our fingertips, but you didn't pick up this book for a cultural diatribe.

You want to make more money. However, you feel as if you are working your butt off merely to make ends meet. You are wondering if it ever gets any better; if you'll eventually cross the threshold into the realm of successful, profitable, sustainable, manageable and enjoyable business life.

Don't shoot the messenger. The business profits and freedom you've been searching for have been in your business this entire time. The great news is that they are still there, hiding just out of sight, waiting for you to seize them.

That's what this book is about. It's about finding the customers and thereby the sales that will take your business to the next level.

It's not about some new-fangled, shiny object, though the methods might seem new.

It's not about social media fads, though you'll likely use your feeds.

It's not about offering new products, though you might.

It's about taking the assets you already have, the customers you already have, the products you already have, the marketing you are already doing, the software you are already using, and leveraging all that existing stuff into real business growth.

You are not supposed to do all 47 things. You should read through them all, however. You should complete all the worksheets, but it is just *impossible* to implement all 47, and that's OK.

Just *one* of these ideas can turn into $1,000, $10,000, even $28,000 when put into action (as it did for my buddy, Ryan, in our Sunflower Mastermind Group). So, pick *one* to implement, completely, the whole way, get it working, then choose your next one.

THERE ARE ONLY 3 WAYS TO BUILD YOUR BUSINESS

- ✓ Get MORE guests
- ✓ Get each guest to pay MORE
- ✓ Get each guest to visit MORE OFTEN

This is important information because we are all starved for time and thus can only choose a limited number of things to do.

Growing a business, whether new or existing, seems like an impossible challenge because it appears that there are an unaccountable number of ways to work at, in, and on your business.

Luckily, to grow your business, there are only these three ways. Every single action you take should pass through this 3-way filter to bring clarity to your effort. You have to know which of these three things you are trying to accomplish *before* you start the work.

Most importantly, you must understand that you can only work on *one* of the ways at a time.

To clarify: Any effort to grow your business must focus on *one* of the ways to grow your business.

Get *more* guests or people or customers. We call our ticket-buying customers 'guests' because Disney

Theme Parks taught that this change in terminology creates a change in behavior. You treat a 'guest' differently than you treat a 'customer'. In your business, call people what you like, but know that you need *more* customers.

Get each customer to pay *more*. This is also known as increasing the average sale, increasing the share of customer, or simply raising your prices. You are not working for more customers, but instead to increase the revenue per customer.

Get customers to shop/purchase/visit more often. Know the quickest way to double sales? Get every customer to visit twice as often. By merely visiting your coffee shop twice a week instead of once a week, you've just increased the value of the customer by 100%.

If you run a seasonal business, such as our corn maze, we need our guests to visit again for Christmas trees, and then we will have doubled the guest's value.

As you work through this book and start planning how to use the best ideas for you, use this filter to clarify the goal of your ad, promotion, incentive, or marketing effort.

There are only three ways to grow your business. Which are you using in your current promotion?

NO ONE KNOWS WHO YOU ARE, WHERE YOU ARE, AND WHAT YOU DO

In the book *Made to Stick*, Chip and Dan Heath refer to "The Curse of Knowledge." They describe this curse as a state in which, because we, the business owner, know all the details about our products and businesses, we thus assume that each and every person to whom we are marketing has the same level of knowledge about our products, services, and activities.

This is dead wrong. People everywhere, including our current customers, think primarily about themselves. In fact, they may *never* think of your business until something reminds them.

Regarding marketing, this is a game-changer. Go back and review some of your advertisements. Review some of your emails. Review your parking lot signage. Review your pricing signs.

Are you marketing, directing, selling, or communicating in a way that assumes your customers have advance, remembered, or prior knowledge of your products, services, or store? I bet you are.

My favorite example of this is listening to agritourism farmers talk about the "Parking Lot Disaster" when the "General Public" comes to "My Farm." How come "None of them know how to park?!"

The kicker: "Any idiot would be able to figure this out!"

It's a classic case of each farmer, me included, who knows exactly where, when, and how we'd like our parking lot utilized for maximum efficiency during a busy corn maze weekend.

Absolutely *zero* of our customers got the memo that included parking lot plans and diagrams, common traffic flow patterns, handicapped space locations, or access control protocols. None of them are idiots. No customer wants to feel stupid. They do not possess the prior knowledge that you as the owner possess.

The real question is this:

> What have you, as the owner or manager of the business, done to make each piece of marketing – each ad, the layout of your parking lot, your market shelves, the choices of beef, the French fry options – as simple, understandable, and complete with the desired action step evident to someone with no prior knowledge?

If you start each idea from this book with the understanding that no one knows who you are, where you are, and what you do, your messages to the customer will cut through the clutter and make it easy for each customer to do business with you.

SELL ONE THING TO ONE PERSON AT A TIME

You can only sell one thing to one person at a time.

"But wait!" you say. "I have 143 products in my store! I have to sell more than one thing at a time!"

More choices are better, right? I mean, if you try to sell one thing, and your customer doesn't want that one thing, then you've lost a customer, right?

Not exactly. In the fantastic book on choice architecture *Nudge* by Thaler and Sunstein, the authors propose that too many choices essentially result in the default choice being *"No Choice"* or *"None of the Above."*

Here's an example from radio advertising. Try to picture the ideal customer targeted by this ad copy:

> *"Hey gang, it's Big Willie from Big Willie's Farm. You gotta get out here. Bring Grandma, Grandpa, Mom, Dad, the kids, their friends, and everybody in-between because we've got a jumping pillow, hayride, pumpkins, animals, farm market, bakery, farm-style games, apple picking, and even more! This is Big Willie, and we're all having fun down on the farm!"*

This ad is riddled with mistakes to "throw everything against the wall and see what sticks." Ads like this are easy for tired ad salespeople to write because they can go to your website and read off a list of everything you have. Next, they try to broaden the net of potential prospects by listing everyone from Grandma to your kid's friends.

This example is about as far from selling one thing to one person at one time as you can get and this ad is tragically typical. In fact, maybe you have one of these running right now...

Let's help Big Willie and create an example with a clearly defined audience and offer:

> *"Hey moms! Do you have a darling little preschooler who loves baby animals? This week, we are featuring "Mommy & Me Meet the Babies" at Big Willie's Kiddie Barnyard. It's a day full of "Ooos, Ahhs and Awes" as your little tyke meets the newest crop of barnyard buddies in our Animal Babies experience area. Learn from our retired teachers as you get the absolutely cutest pictures of your little ones with our little ones. See you at Big Willie's 'Mommy & Me Meet the Babies' in the corral daily from 9AM-2PM."*

Now how does this ad differ from the first? The target is clearly moms of preschoolers who have time from 9AM-2PM. It is selling only one thing: "Mommy & Me Meet the Babies."

Can you see the difference? It is crucially important that as you implement the ideas in this book, you focus on selling one thing at one time to one person.

LIFETIME CUSTOMER VALUE

I have been short-sighted in regard to Lifetime Customer Value at the Maize Quest Corn Maze & Fun Park. Maybe you have been short-sighted in your business, too.

When I ask, "What's a customer worth to your business?" you would very likely picture a typical day, typical customer walking in the door, selecting merchandise, perhaps visiting an orchard to pick fruit, walking up to purchase tickets, or taking the routine actions that precede a sale.

Next, you might look in their cart or bag or basket and add up the amount they are likely to spend. It could be $23, $54, or even $113. Then, your brain returns the cumulative total as the answer.

For Maize Quest, the average family spends $12 on each ticket, then another $3-5 per person on snack foods, so a customer is worth about $15-$17, right?

Wrong. Dead wrong.

Because the customer interaction is immediate, when they hand you the money, ordinarily we only think about the quick transaction. We believe the customer is worth only the value of the current purchase.

But, it is critical to know what a customer is really worth. In my case, it's that customer's initial spending at Maize Quest, Maple Lawn Farms, and

Maple Lawn Winery *combined*, but it doesn't stop there.

To find the real value of a customer at our business, we need to change our perspective again to encompass a full year's worth of spending. In the diagram, we show that instead of the original $15-17, a single customer could be worth up to $809.

Incremental Sales
What's ONE guest worth?

Total $809

Group Booking Spend

Annual Wine Spend

CSA Spend

Admission Spend
Pumpkin Spend
Cider & Donut Spend
PYO Apple Spend

$15 $16 $35 $48 $297 $128 $270

Change perspective to the Lifetime Value of the customer and diagram 2 shows that one customer could be worth $3,236 over four years.

Lifetime Value
What's ONE guest REALLY worth?

$809	$809	$809	$809	=$3,236
Year 1	Year 2	Year 3	Year 4	

What would you do to get this guest?

Change perspective one more time, and we see that the Multiplier Growth value of a single customer could be worth thousands and thousands of dollars due to referrals, bringing friends and friends of friends.

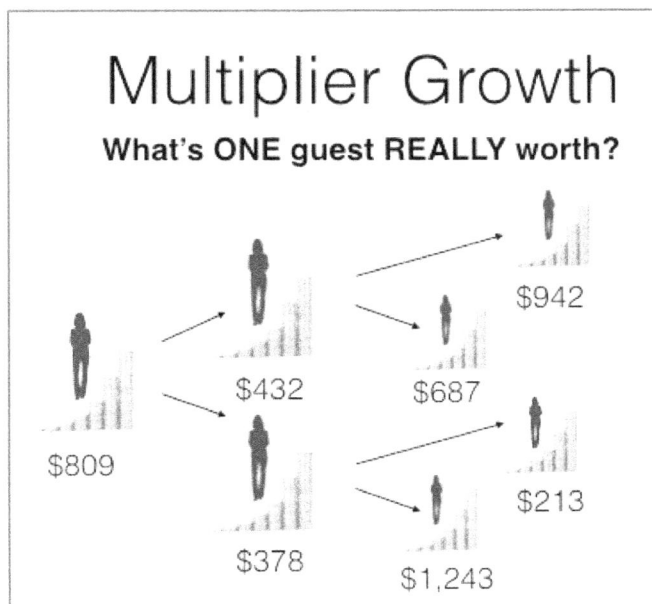

Multiplier Growth
What's ONE guest REALLY worth?

$809

$432

$378

$687

$942

$213

$1,243

We must zoom out from our narrow, transactional view and see that all the revenue we need for our businesses is out there. Your customers have more money than they are spending now. Your customers have friends who have money, and so do their friends.

As you implement the ideas in this book, challenge yourself to determine the actual Lifetime Customer Value for a customer in your business. With this more accurate number, you can take the long view in planning your strategy for growth.

View this FREE Video on Lifetime Customer Value, as part of "The Cross-Marketing Multiplier." www.HughMcPherson.com/MoreCustomers

Destination Visitor vs. Weekly Shopper

In the discussion of Lifetime Customer Value, it is crucial that you segment your clientele into Destination Visitor or Weekly Shopper.

Destination Visitors (DVs) have some characteristics relevant to the way you approach marketing to them. They typically only visit you once per season, and maybe only once per year.

Surely you know of customers anecdotally who arrive for pick-your-own strawberries, have a beautiful day, take lots of pictures, grab a snack, have a picnic, then pack up the car and say, "See you next year!" Those are your DV customers.

DVs typically spend more during the visit to your business, because it is an annual tradition and they will not be returning. They need to 'get it all today' because, in their minds, there is no 'tomorrow.'

Weekly Shoppers (WSs) are critically different. Imagine you have a farmer's market stand each Thursday morning in town. Your WSs come to visit your booth each week to get their fresh produce for the week. They walk down the market and wave as they say, "See you next week!"

Marketing to WSs is wildly different than marketing to DVs. Loyalty, recognition, and knowing their names, all go much further than a Groupon for a one-time-offer of 50%OFF.

WSs build Lifetime Customer Value more quickly than DVs. If they are spending even just $20 per week at your market booth, in two months a single person will be worth over $160, and over a 20-week run a WS could spend over $400.

No matter how good you are at selling a 'big day' to a DV, the WS is more valuable over time. Knowing this, what would you pay to gain a $400 farmer's market customer?

The ultimate category is Daily Shoppers (DSs). Starbucks works hard to make you into a DS. Wouldn't it be great if someone came to your business and shopped with you every day?

Imagine a scenario in which you are a farmer's market vendor with lots of WS customers, and you hold a "Day with the Farmer" ticketed event at your farm for one weekend. You would be changing WSs to DVs for a weekend, thus enhancing profitability.

Imagine that you operate a Fall Harvest corn maze and festival, but at the festival, you offer coupons for your new Christmas gift basket product line. You would be making a DV into a DVx2.

Imagine that you operate a strawberry patch, but make the most incredible Strawberry Jam. At the patch, you launch an online store to your DVs to subscribe to a Jar of the Month club. You would be making WSs of your DVs.

What is your primary category for customers?

Do you have both kinds of customers?

Can you convert DVs to WSs?

Can you change a WS into an occasional DV?

What current products or experiences are marketable to each category of customer?

Take a minute to list your answers below.

_____

_____

_____

_____

_____

_____

_____

THE GREAT WALL OF HABITUAL ACTIONS

"We are what we repeatedly do. Excellence, then, is not an act, but a habit." – Will Durant

In working to market your business and gain new customers, you are about to hit a wall. It is not one of the walls you thought you'd run into, such as competitors, pricing, time to do your marketing, Facebook's algorithm, apathetic Millennials, or technology.

You are about to run into The Great Wall of Habitual Actions.

Think about it. You likely shop in the same supermarket, for the same items, from the same shelves in the same order, on the same day of the week.

You likely drive the same way, to the same dentist, on your way to the same barbershop.

Nine out of the last ten movies you've seen were likely in the same Cineplex.

Why? Because you and your brain are lazy.

In his book *The Power of Habit: Why We Do What We Do in Life and Business*, Charles Duhigg proposes that because our ancestors were perpetually short on calories to survive, and the brain is the biggest consumer of calories in the body by weight, our brains developed habits as a form of energy conservation.

This conservation of energy in the brain means that when you zone out listening to music or a podcast as you are driving on a familiar road, you are in less danger than a newly minted teenage driver because you have cemented in your brain the pattern for safely driving that road.

It also means that we are more likely to do what we have always done, because doing something new requires our brain to use the executive functions of prefrontal cortex, at a high cost of calories, to make executive decisions regarding the new information.

Test my theory. Have you ever had an event in your business marketing life in which you were so busy when the advertising rep called to set up an appointment that you simply said, "You know what? Let's do the same thing we did last year"?

By 'doing what you did last year,' your brain just wholly avoided using all that energy to learn about new options in advertising. Your brain avoided the time it would take to dig into Facebook Event Advertising to figure out how to target flower freaks in Oshkosh to attend your tulip festival. Your brain defaulted to the well-worn groove... to the habit.

The brain's ability to move repetitive tasks from executive function to thoughtless habit is a great feature. You do not want to use your executive function to tie-up the 4,373rd bag of kettle korn. You want some things to be on autopilot.

Habitual autopilot is a terrible, horrible, no good, very bad brain feature in *every single one of your future customers* as it relates to you while you work to grow your business.

Every potential customer is too busy, meaning every customer's mind is already working overtime to protect itself from utilizing executive functions. Every customer's brain has erected The Great Wall of Habitual Actions around his or her life with daily routines that do not include you.

That means you have to do something to tear down that wall.

Some examples:

- Groupon flourished early on because giving its list holders a crazy 50%OFF discount was so wild, it would get customers to try that new salon, zip line, or bistro.

- Reality TV was fresh, shocking, and voyeuristic compared to the standard scripted dramas and laugh-track sitcoms of the day.

- Facebook LIVE videos were so novel two years ago, and people would share them like crazy, even mid-stream, merely to be a part of the action.

- Dropping a giant pumpkin from a crane was a wild craze for a few years.

- Drone footage was incredibly engaging 3-4 years ago because it provided a vantage point unlike any seen to date.

- Zombie Paintball was so unusual and immersive that it swept the nation as the TV show "The Walking Dead" blew up on cable.

- Sunflower fields have captivated people for years, but only recently have farms welcomed guests in, instead of shooing them away.

Each example cracks through this Great Wall of Habitual Actions using novelty, the intensity of experience, exclusivity, extreme discounting, or personal connection to shock or move potential customers out of their daily routines to try something new.

You are part of your own growth problem. You want things to stay the same, and though this book has lots of new ideas, each idea looks like a big hassle to your brain. Your mind is actually working against you!

The only remedy is to do some serious, written goal setting. Once your goals are in writing, then you need to set just one small habit per day – to read your goals to yourself in the morning.

To help you in this regard, I've included with your book a FREE online course called "A Goal Without A Plan Is A Wish" *and* all the printouts and goal worksheets I use throughout the year.

If you set your goal in mind, commit it to paper and review it daily, your brain will start working for you, instead of against you. Your mind will begin seeking ways to complete the goal even when you are unaware of its processing.

You can break down The Great Wall of Habitual Actions in the minds of your customers using the plans in this book.

Just make sure to start by tearing down your own wall.

FREE online course included for readers:

"A Goal Without A Plan Is A Wish"

The habits we just referenced above start with goals. However, a goal without a plan is merely a wish. After this course, you'll have the tools you need to make goal achievement a process, a habit.

So...

Why are written goals so important?

Why is willpower not enough to achieve?

Why are you struggling every year with the same issues?

Our "Goal without a plan is a Wish" online workshop is totally FREE, because it is so incredibly important for your success.

In this course, you move through a process for goal setting using our templates and examples, so you can add powerful reasons WHY to your goals, so the goal itself pulls you toward completion.

Get it for FREE at:
www.HughMcPherson.com/MoreCustomers

IGNORE YOUR COMPETITORS

"The farm down the street has 15 attractions and charges $10 per person. We only have 11 attractions, so I guess I'll charge $8 per person."

"The bakery at Smith's sells five cookies for $3.00, so we'll sell five cookies for $2.75 and get all their business."

"There are four farms in this end of the county, and no one has gone up from $15 per half-bushel of apples in the past ten years. If we increase our price, we'll lose everything."

"They got a bouncy pillow, so we better get one next year, or we're sunk."

I can't say this in strong enough language...

You need to ignore your competitors.

I know that you don't believe me. You might be able to quote your college economics professor who waxed poetic about supply and demand and fungible widgets, but that clown was dead wrong.

You need to ignore your competitors.

What if you are the 'Big Dog' business in your category in your area? What do you have to fear from a scrappy competitor? Ignore them.

What if you are the scrappy little guy trying to make a name for yourself? Can you in any way keep up with your 'Big Dog' in terms of marketing money, attraction building, or the number of home-made pie flavors? Nope, so ignore them.

When you fight with your competitors, real or imagined, you are expending mental energy and time. You need all the mental energy and time you can get to work on your own business, so ignore them.

Have you ever been jealous of a competitor even when you know you don't want to be like them? I have a farm market near me that is so incredibly, irritatingly near-and-dear to (seemingly) everyone's hearts. They are also open 364.5 days of the year, which I *never* want to do. Waste of energy, ignore your competitors.

In the big picture, we, you, me, my business, your business, and all our competitors' operations, are so infinitesimal in the grand scheme of the total dollars floating around in our respective geographic areas, that any change in any of those small businesses simply... doesn't... matter.

What matters is what you do to improve your business.

What matters is how hard you work to train your staff.

What matters is how clever and innovative you can be as you connect with your customers.

What matters is how hard you work to expand your customer base.

What matters is focusing on the quality of experience your customer has when you are lucky enough to have her cross your threshold.

So stop obsessing over your competitors. It is a pointless waste of your valuable time and mental resources.

Ignore your competitors. You have absolutely no control over them.

Instead, exert your mental energy on something you can control. Focus on making changes to your business and yourself.

30,000-Foot Marketing Flight Plan

This book is a reference guide, a set of tools you will deploy at the ground-level. Open the book and get to work. Nothing is stopping you!

If you'd like a 30,000-ft, big-picture flight plan for your marketing, please preview – for FREE – our online course: The Event Tsunami.

The Event Tsunami is the flight plan. We layout for you EXACTLY what you should be doing 120 Days, 90 Days, 60 Days, and 30 Days before your special event, your opening, your product launch, your festival, or your farm-to-table dinner.

This guide is NOT ideas or theory, it is a full set of templates, checklists, schedules, scripts, press releases, and how-to guides to help you make the most out of your hard work... and get the MOST out of your events.

Every tool in THIS book, will hang neatly on the Event Tsunami framework. PLUS, readers of this book may save 30% OFF our premier marketing course: The Event Tsunami with promo code: CC30

If you're ready to get the full plan, visit: www.HughMcPherson.com/MoreCustomers

Now, let's fill that toolbox.

Focus Area 1

Grow Your Customer List

➤➤➤➤

"He who has the biggest list, wins." —Lisa Jiminez

It would be wonderful if every customer you added in a year, stayed, so you could start the next year with all your previous customers and grow from there.

But that is not the way of the marketing world. You probably overestimate the number of return customers you'll see in any given week, month, season, or year.

Customers come. Customers leave. Customers get sick. Customers die. Customers move away. Customers forget. Customers get mad. Customers age out of your preschool tour program. Customers get wrapped up in their busy lives.

There are a hundred reasons why at any time, any customer might stop transacting business with you. In fact, you are losing customers right now!

But don't panic, there is a natural attrition rate in any business.

That is why you have to work to build your customer list consistently. By consistently, imagine that you add just 10 customers a week throughout the year. You'd have 520 new customers a year. Add a single customer to your list each day? 365 new customers. If you are a seasonal business, you might add 200 customers a week for 15 weeks – that's 3,000 new customers!

However, these customers aren't going to flock to your business without focused effort on your part.

Take a minute and list the ways you work to add customers to your list currently:

_____

_____

_____

_____

_____

_____

Typically, when I ask this question, business owners list off the ways they advertise. While advertising is helpful, *it is not the same as* building your customer list.

The ideas in this section focus on building your customer list, because...

"She who has the biggest list, wins."

1. Collect Leads – Online Contest

No one wants your stupid email newsletter. That's what I found out the hard way. For years after email marketing became fashionable with early programs such as Constant Contact, business owners like me put a little box in the corner of our websites with a chipper message to "Sign-up for our eNewsletter!"

Sign up to our newsletter

Email Address

[   ] *

First Name

[   ]

Last Name

[   ]

Subscribe

Why? Well, for a while, it worked! It worked until email grew from novelty to daily use and spammers jammed our customers' inboxes. I would hazard a guess that the LAST thing any of my customers now want is my "eNewsletter."

Or so they think...

People are happy to get things for FREE. People LOVE to 'WIN.' To keep people signing up for your email list, it takes a simple change to the wording on your website.

Using built-in sign-up forms in all major email service providers (such as Mail Chimp, Constant Contact, AWeber, iContact or similar service), change the text on the sign-up form from "Join our email newsletter" to "Enter for a Chance to WIN!"

To install, follow the email service instructions or have your website person add the form to the top right corner of your website, directly under the header. This location is one of the highest viewed areas on websites.

Test the form with your email once installed to make sure it works.

The prize can be a family four-pack of tickets, a Christmas tree, a spring gardening package, a month of free coffee, or any other prize that makes sense for your business.

Keep these tips in mind as you complete this project:

- Ask ONLY for "First Name" & "Email" in your form. Asking for less information lowers the barrier for completion. You want a LOT of names.

- List the Value – BIG prizes = More entrants. "Chance to WIN a Fall Decorative Package ($300 VALUE!)" Always list the full retail value to entice more entrants.

- Give away prizes regularly. People like to WIN. You need people to get excited. You want lots of entrants to grow your list. You need social media posts. So... Pick Winners! As advertising goes, this prize package costs you almost nothing, so leverage what you already have and create winners.

- When you pick winners, make a BIG deal out of it. Announce winners LIVE on Facebook. Send pictures of winners picking up their prizes in your email newsletters. Post winners' photos on Instagram.

CHECKLIST

Collect Leads – Online Contest

✓ Sign up for an email service provider

✓ Create a sign-up form

✓ Add sign-up form to the website

View our FREE list of tools and software we use for our lead capture system at:

www.HughMcPherson.com/MoreCustomers

2. Collect Leads On-site as Ticket

Pie is powerful. Pie has the power to separate personal information from guests. Yes, we have used pies to get customer names, emails, addresses, and mobile phone numbers.

Building your list online is excellent, but you may have plenty of customers come through the door of your business, have a great time, then depart without ever identifying themselves to you. Most often they depart without leaving any way to connect.

So, at your next event, you are going to collect customer information in place of an admission ticket.

EXAMPLE 1: Group Leader Open House

We love booking groups of scouts, schools, and church youth for our corn maze. To entice new leaders and reward leaders who booked in previous years, we hold an annual Group Leader Open House (GLOH) about a month before we open the maze for the season.

Admission to the GLOH is FREE for the leader and up to 6 guests, BUT ONLY if the leaders pre-register online with all their information including: Name, phone, address, email, group type and more.

If they just show up at the event and are not on the pre-registration list, they must fill out the information before we relinquish the tickets.

EXAMPLE 2: *Holiday Pie Tasting*

To boost Thanksgiving Week pie sales, we held a Holiday Pie Tasting event. Admission was free, but only if you completed the "Holiday Pie Tasting Rating & Order Sheet."

Pie Taster Information – (1) per sheet, please

First Name:

Last Name:

Email Address:

Mobile Phone:

Street Address:

City: State: Zip:

Your information will NEVER be sold or shared. We love you too much!

Your Round of Holiday Pie Tasting is FREE with this completed information and pie rating sheet.

☑ Please use this sheet to give feedback on the pie AND as your order sheet.

☑ Should you NOT wish to order pies *(which is, frankly, VERY unlikely)*, simply turn in with no quantity selected at the checkout register with your other items today as a survey.

Guess what? 100% of the people entering the farm market completed the "Holiday Pie Tasting Rating & Order Sheet" because it was required to eat the pie samples. It was their ticket!

Post-pie sampling, we now know all the guest information, including their favorite pie flavors.

QUESTIONS

Collect Leads On-site as Ticket

✓ What can you offer as a FREE experience, sampling, or preview for which the only 'admission' is completing a personal information form?

✓ How would you promote the event?

✓ What other questions, such as pie tasting feedback, could you ask to deepen your customer knowledge?

3. Collect Leads On-site as Survey

Online reviews are all the rage, but on-site surveys still have a place in business today. (On-site surveys might even let angry customers blow off some steam before they get back to the Twitter-verse.)

Collecting customer data through a survey is a combination of "Collecting Names Online" and "Collecting Names as a Ticket." You are asking for their name and their feedback in return for a chance to win a prize.

MAIZE QUEST FALL SURVEY

Enter to Win A T-Shirt!

NAME_____DATE_____

ADDRESS_____

CITY_____STATE_____ZIP_____

PH_____EMAIL_____
HOW DID YOU HEAR ABOUT US THIS YEAR? PLEASE CIRCLE
I-83 WELCOME CENTER   WEBSITE   MLF BROCHURE
VISITORS BUREAU   CHURCH   98 YCR/RADIO
YORK DAILY RECORD   BEEN HERE BEFORE?   101.9 WLIF or MIX 106.5

CHECKLIST

Collect Leads On-site as Survey

✓ Customer information. Grab all you can! If you don't ask and leave a blank for the answer, you cannot possibly get it, so ask for EVERYTHING.

✓ How did you hear about us? Make this section as simple as circling from a list of everywhere you advertise or promote.

✓ What did you like best? You might get some great testimonials out of this section.

✓ Where could we improve? Allow space for complaints here so that you can uncover weak spots and address them. This space also lets them get the negativity out of their systems.

✓ Other questions that are relevant to your specific business. We often ask about new games or attractions.

✓ THANK YOU Section. Thank the customers for their time and feedback.

Welcome Sequence – Introductions & Offers

Now that you are collecting new customers and growing your list, you need to take action to turn those new customers and prospective customers into regular customers.

Introductions. Keep in mind that none of your new customers know anything about you. Likely, some of your best customers don't know everything about your product line, and the majority of the customers between those two extremes are missing out on key services you provide.

You need to introduce your new prospects to your business directly.

What happens when you sign up for more information online or at a trade show or at a new business you visit? Often you get one email that says, "Thanks for signing up for our email list." After that, you might get the occasional newsletter – a newsletter in which it is assumed you know what Spring Perennials are and why you care that they are 10%OFF in May.

Utterly terrible.

Consider this: Why do you do business with any business? With a local business? With a small business? Why do customers return to your business? It's very likely that you could go out of business today and no one would go hungry, stop having fun with their families, or go cold turkey on caffeine.

Customers choose you because of relationships and familiarity. The Welcome Sequence is all about building the relationship with your prospective customers and deepening it with your current customers.

The Welcome Sequence is a series of five to seven emails released over time with the specific goal to build a personal relationship with the customer while leading the customer on a focused tour of your business.

Each email focuses on the story behind your business and your products. Each email also provides a substantial offer to try a particular product, service, or event.

Introductions & Offers from the Maple Lawn Farms Welcome Sequence

- Email 1 Intro to: The McPherson Family
- Email 1 Offer: $5 off $30 purchase at the farm
- Email 2 Intro to: Pick Your Own Fruit
- Email 2 Offer: Decorative wooden picking baskets FREE when you pick (2) half bushels of peaches.
- Email 3 Intro to: Farm Market Bakery
- Email 3 Offer: FREE Bag of Kettle Korn with your first pie purchase
- Email 4 Intro to: Maple Lawn Winery
- Email 4 Offer: FREE Wine Tasting with your first visit
- Email 5 Intro to: Maize Quest Corn Maze & Fun Park

- Email 5 Offer: FREE Cider & Donut Treat with ticket purchase
- Email 6 Intro: Sunflower Festival
- Email 6 Offer: FREE Metal Bucket for picking with purchase of two or more tickets.

Email timing. To develop a relationship takes time. To increase the time your new guests are interacting with your business, emails need to be spaced out. After the initial form is filled out, a survey is collected, or an event sheet is completed and turned in, we recommend sending email on this schedule:

Instant, then 24 hours, then three days after that, then five days after that, seven days, and finally 14 days after that. (Note each timing happens after the previous email is sent, NOT from the initial start date.)

This Welcome Sequence creates a total of 6 connections over your new customer's first 30 days, giving the new customer the opportunity to get to know you. If you are concerned that you'll never remember to send all those emails to each person every time, you are correct.

You should, but you won't. The solution to this problem is the subject of the next section.

CHECKLIST

Introductions & Offers Welcome Sequence

Create introduction content and specific offers for:

- ✓ Email 1 Intro to:

- ✓ Email 1 Offer:

- ✓ Email 2 Intro to:

- ✓ Email 2 Offer:

- ✓ Email 3 Intro to:

- ✓ Email 3 Offer:

- ✓ Email 4 Intro to:

- ✓ Email 4 Offer:

- ✓ Email 5 Intro to:

- ✓ Email 5 Offer:

- ✓ Email 6 Intro to:

- ✓ Email 6 Offer to:

View a FREE Social Advertising DECODED
Course overview video at:

www.HughMcPherson.com/MoreCustomers

Welcome Sequence – Automation

Executing the Welcome Sequence follow-up emails with introductions and offers sounds impossible. How could you possibly send emails at the right time for each person, no matter when they signed up? You'd need a full-time person just to do that, right? Nope.

Hire robots. Fortunately, repetitive tasks are the bread and butter of robots. Most email marketing services now offer the ability to set up automated campaigns called autoresponders. It is often an increase in your monthly fee, but to extract the benefits of a fully functioning Welcome Sequence, it's worth it.

Your basic outline is to set a timer to trigger the next email to send to your customer for the correct delay following the previous email or customer action.

Email, timer, email 2, timer 2, etc. as depicted in the diagram from our online class Social Advertising: DECODED.

Social Advertising:DECODED Module 6

Email Campaign Name: *Winery Welcome Series* What is this campaign trying to do? *Intro Products*

Subject: Welcome to the Winery, Bread Special
Action: Push next weekend visit

Delay: 1 day

Subject: Fields of Joy
Action: Sell Sunflower Fest Tickets

Delay: 3 days

CHECKLIST

Welcome Sequence Automation

✓ Log in to your email marketing platform and search for 'autoresponders' or 'campaign' options.

✓ Sign up for the enhanced service if it is not included in your package.

✓ Copy and paste your first email text and pictures from the Welcome Sequence chapter, or, if you have already built them in your email marketing platform, choose to use them in your new campaign.

✓ Set the timer.

✓ Repeat for the next email & timer.

FOCUS AREA 2

CRM MARKETING USING YOUR CUSTOMER LIST

Introduction

Use what you already have; the tools you've already got. That's the subtitle of this book. To be efficient at growing your business, the Artificial Intelligence firm SumAll studied over 815,000 transactions to look at the effect of marketing to existing customers for repeat sales.

After a customer purchases one time, that customer has only a 27% chance of buying again. However, after purchasing three times, the customer's likelihood of returning increases to 54%.[1]

After focusing on building your customer list and collecting the existing customers into a file, this

---

[1] https://blog.sumall.com/journal/the-importance-of-repeat-customers-2.html

focus area moves into the realm of Customer Relationship Management or CRM.

Each tactic uses tools to connect and incentivize repeat business – repeated connections between you and your customers. Now that we've got your customers, let's work to activate them on a regular basis.

Direct mail by interest

If you were alive in the 1980s, you might remember your full mailbox. The mailbox used to be stuffed to the brim with direct mail, catalogs, Publisher's Clearing House offers, and sales letters.

It was full of junk mail.

Then along came email in the late '90s and, since it was virtually free, the physical mailbox began to decline in importance to marketers as they reduced costs by going electronic.

Now the U.S. Postal Service has fallen on lean times, and your mailbox volume is dwindling. This thin stack of mail is excellent news for marketing your business.

The U.S.P.S.'s data indicates that 98% of people check their mailbox every day,[2] and 77% of people sort their mail as soon as it arrives.[3] That means your message has a high probability of being seen as soon as it arrives.

Direct mail is more expensive than email, but with a 98% viewer rate, and 77% viewing rate on day one, it is an effective way to build repeat business and drive customers back to your business.

It is also a lot easier than it used to be to send targeted direct mail to a list of customers. If you are

---

[2]http://www.pb.com/docs/US/pdf/Microsite/Nonprofit/ed_np_getyourmailopened_05MailMoment.pdf

[3] Consumer Channel Preference Study, Epsilon, 2015.

targeting your best customers, it can also be the most profitable.

Mailing success depends on building your customer list to include mailing addresses. In the Cross-Marketing Focus Area, we cover in-depth methods to encourage and automatically capture this data from your customers.

Use services such as VistaPrint.com and Postcardbuilder.com to easily upload artwork or use templates to create offer postcards. Next, upload your customer list with mailing addresses, then click send.

That's it. Your message, branding, and compelling offers will physically arrive in your customers' hands within 7-10 days.

Loyalty Program

A basic loyalty program rewards a customer for repeat visits or for reaching spending thresholds. Loyalty programs can be as simple as a paper punch card.

Most familiar to me was the local pizzeria punch cards with "Buy nine pizzas, get the 10th pizza FREE."

Now, possibly the most successful loyalty program of all time is the Starbucks mobile app with over 14.9 million monthly users,[4] gaining "Starbucks Stars" with every pricey coffee purchase, and playing games that reward multiple visits in a weekend. (Full disclosure, I have the same account logged in on my wife's phone as well as my own, so we gain stars faster.)

The point is that encouraging, training, entertaining, and growing repeat customers is valuable and need not be a high-tech challenge. By having any loyalty program, you create connections with customers and increase their likelihood of returning to your business.

Key to the program is determining what you want to track. Do you want to track dollars spent, or visits to your store? Track bagels purchased, or season pass visits?

---

[4]https://www.recode.net/2018/5/22/17377234/starbucks-mobile-payments-users-apple-pay-google

Each business has different goals, so you want to use the program to track the 'bread and butter' purchases, then reward with the unexpected or new products.

For instance, you might track a customer's weekly dollar purchases at your farmer's market stand and when they hit $100, instead of a coupon for 5% OFF, why not delight him with one of your signature "Monster Cookies"?

If you track baskets of apples purchased throughout your Fall Harvest season, why not reward with a bottle of wine from your winery?

If you track ticket purchases for your corn maze or attractions, you could reward with a half-pound of fudge from your market.

Each Loyalty Reward moves your customers to a different part of your business.

CHECKLIST

Loyalty Program

✔ What items or categories are profitable that you can track?

✔ How will you track them? (paper, punch card, phone app, in your POS system)

✔ How much purchase generates how much reward?

✔ How will you train your staff to encourage the collection of punches or stars?

✔ How will you train your staff to deliver and track rewards efficiently?

Phone-based Loyalty App Examples:

Stampme.com
Flok.com
Fivestars.com/businesses

Point-Of-Sale Loyalty App Examples:

Squareup.com
Clover.com
Talech.com

View our FREE list of tools and software we use for Loyalty Systems at:

www.HughMcPherson.com/MoreCustomers

Unlock Your POS as a CRM – Square

Point Of Sale (POS) systems are readily available and relatively affordable. The most economical versions run as apps on iPads or Android devices. The POS system replaces older-style cash registers.

You need the data. If you haven't made the jump to POS from old cash registers, you are missing a lot of information and wasting a lot of time with older machines.

We found that the reports alone gave us the insight and time savings to justify the purchase of the equipment. The speed of balancing register drawers or tills saves valuable back office time.

To save on the initial investment, we purchased refurbished iPads from Amazon's Warehouse site for $150-$200 each, bought the printers on eBay, and started with the basic level software, in this case, Squareup.com.

Once you are set with the basic system, turning your POS into a Customer Relationship Management tool starts creating value. As your customers swipe credit cards to pay for purchases, your POS is capturing their contact data automatically.

As we learned in Focus Area 1, building your List is of utmost importance, your POS can take on some of those actions. Square is not the only POS service to contain a CRM tool, but it is FREE to start and is a popular platform for small businesses.

Once up and running, click "Customers" on the left menu bar to take a look through the data collected by Square. Using a POS starts the process of building your internal "customers-who-have-bought-from-you" database.

Note that your customer database from your POS is different from your email newsletter list in that marketing to your POS database should be focused on building repeat business, not on completing the first sale.

Automate Square POS Campaigns

The real power in using Square or any POS system is in automating the marketing tasks you know you should perform, but never have time to complete. Again, Square is merely our example.

Note that these automated campaigns do require an additional service fee paid to Square. Please check current pricing online. Compared to the extra expense and knowing that I'd never get this done on my own, I view the fee as a good value.

Automated campaigns

In the Square Marketing module, there are six primary campaigns to set up. Each campaign, once in place, runs automatically for each customer who qualifies to receive the campaign emails or actions.

Here's a description of each campaign from Square's Support site:

- o Welcome: This email is sent to new customers within 24 hours of their first purchase and encourages them to come back again.

- o Win-back: This email is sent to lapsed customers. Your lapsed customers are those who've made three purchases within a 6-month period but haven't returned in the last six weeks. This message is meant to bring them back.

o Birthday Offer: This email automatically sends a coupon to each customer seven days before their birthday.

o Birthday Collector: If you're missing birthdays for some of your customers, this campaign will help you collect them. This email will ask up to 50 customers per day if they want to share their birthday with you, and it will add their birthdays to your Customer Directory when customers opt-in.

o Reputation: This campaign automatically sends an email to any customers who visit your store frequently or have left you feedback through Square receipts. This type of email requires a one-time setup and will continue to be sent until you stop the campaign.

o Build up your Facebook presence: Asks customers to Like you on Facebook after their first sale.

Now imagine that those campaigns had been running for your business throughout the last season. How many emails, birthdays, positive feedback replies, and more social media Likes would you have?

The key is that when you invest some time up front, this system allows you to reap the benefits automatically indefinitely.

Automate Square Loyalty Program

When choosing a POS system, check to see if the system supports a loyalty program. Square offers a Loyalty module for an additional charge. We added it to our winery to track purchases and encourage repeat visits.

With Square's Loyalty module, you set how your customers earn points, similar to those Starbucks Stars. Customers earn points Per Visit, Per Amount Spent or Per Item/Category.

In our winery, we made it super easy. Each bottle of wine or 4-pack of hard cider equals 1 Reward Point. After 12 points, the customer receives a notification that her next purchase is 20%OFF. Simple.

CHECKLIST

POS Loyalty Program

✓ How are points earned?

✓ What tiers earn which kind of reward?

✓ How does the system track it?

✓ How does my staff redeem it?

Keep in mind that the tracking happens automatically through the software after each transaction when the customer inputs her mobile number. The automated marketing campaigns send messages to customers such as "confirmed points awarded by the most recent sale," "almost to an award," "award earned" along with the coupon code that offers the reward.

Redeeming the award is as easy as punching in the code at checkout the next time the customer makes a purchase.

Starbucks will likely remain the king of loyalty programs, but that doesn't mean that we small business people can't provide a way to reward our customers, too.

Bounce Back Extreme Coupon

In the introduction, you learned that the chance of a customer returning for a second sale is just 27%, but increases to 45% after his second visit and up to 54% after three visits.

You need to get that new customer back into the store ASAP. The trick is overcoming the mere 27% likelihood of the customer to return after the first visit.

To overcome this resistance and start building a shopping pattern in the customer, use an Extreme Bounce Back Coupon (EBBC).

Similar to the use of Groupon (which we discuss later in the book), you are going to plan such an outrageous offer that the customer feels as though he or she is going to LOSE money if they DON'T redeem your coupon!

Example 1: You run a restaurant and welcome a new couple in for breakfast. They love the meal and with their change or receipt at the end of breakfast, you present them with a Buy-One-Get-One coupon for lunch.

This coupon serves to entice the diners back for a different meal to help them explore the menu. It promotes the second visit at a ridiculously low price. It's such a crazy offer, the customer is likely to talk about it.

Example 2: You manage a farm produce market. You know that by next week, you are going to be 'up to your ears' in carrots. So, THIS week's artisan cheese buyers receive a coupon for 2 FREE pounds of carrots, redeemable next week. You are rewarding a high-margin item purchase of cheese, planning to get some value out of perishable carrot over-supply by delighting customers, and requiring the customers to return next week, building customer shopping habits.

Example 3: You are trying to create a new event in July, a sunflower festival. You've never been open in July, but you have good traffic for strawberry season in May. You decide to offer (4) FREE tickets to the Sneak Preview Friday of Sunflower Fest, a $40 VALUE, to any family that picks four buckets of strawberries.

A word of caution is necessary for the use of Extreme Bounce Back Coupons. Use EBBCs to encourage only the first return visit of brand NEW customers. The gain in return visits is between the first and second visits of NEW customers. Use EBBCs to launch NEW products, events or 'seasons'. Use EBBCs as a reward for mega-purchasers who make exceptional contributions to your business revenue.

However, repeated use of the EBBC trains a different habit – "Waiting for the Coupon." By definition, deploy an "Extreme" offer sparingly.

CHECKLIST

Extreme Bounce Back Coupon

✓ Determine what customer action you are trying to encourage: Repeat visit to your store? Try out a different product line? Reach a spending level? Launch a new event?

✓ What is the long-term value of the action you are encouraging?

✓ How much can you discount the current transaction to achieve the long-term gain? Examples include launching a new festival successfully with minimal advertising, getting new customers addicted to you macaroons, or subscribing to your mail order honey & tea service.

✓ Will this target NEW customers only?

✓ Will this target seasonal customers to come back in a new season?

✓ Will this be a reward coupon for a mega purchase?

Extreme Bounce Back Coupon: Online from On-site Visit

For local businesses, often we require that customers come to us to purchase. We are the brick and mortar stores. Our farms are destinations that must be experienced. We offer items you cannot buy anywhere else.

In marketing experiences, that is great! It's exclusively ours to deliver on-site. Your store or cafe or farm should be so cool that shopping there could be a ticketed experience!

But so often, the fun and the customer revenue stops dead at the farm gate. Once that customer leaves your property or walks out your door, they stop purchasing. However, the customer doesn't stop spending money. She's just spending money everywhere ELSE.

If you have products that can ship or gift cards for next season, you could add an online component to your business.

We recently launched an online wine store because we are so far away from our customers. We even CLOSE for four months each year, which makes it very difficult for customers to make purchases.

The Extreme Bounce Back Coupon comes into play when pushing customers from visiting the store in person to placing their first order online. If a customer has never placed an online order with you, it is likely she will not.

The EBBC is designed to get your on-site customers to 'take a chance' and use your online store. You may have thousands of on-site visitors who you can treat as NEW customers to your online store.

CHECKLIST

Extreme Bounce Back Coupon
Online from On-site Visit

✓ Choose an offer to entice your on-site visitor into your NEW online store.

✓ Choose products or services to deliver online that make sense for your customers to continue purchasing from home.

✓ Plan how you will reach out to your existing customers to market the offer to make the FIRST online purchase.

Guest Reviews – Ask across sites

Managing guest reviews seems passive. Customers visit, and when they leave, maybe they write a review, maybe they don't.

Asking for reviews feels somewhat dangerous or even disingenuous. If I ask for a review, isn't that cheating? If they felt strongly enough to give us a good review, wouldn't they have already written it? What if I ask and they write a bad review?

All those feelings are false, and based in a fearful or 'scarcity' mindset. If you are doing an excellent job for your customers, then they should be delighted to write a review about your business.

So ask!

When we completed the sign-up for TripAdvisor and claimed our listing, we went through adding pictures, writing descriptions, completing forms and did the entire account set-up.

When we pulled up our new listing, we found nothing. Nada. No stars. We needed some reviews and interactions, or it would look like we were either fake or unimportant. So, I went to Facebook and announced, "We are now officially on Trip Advisor, and if you loved Maize Quest, and have a free minute or two, could you share your experience with other Trip Advisor users?"

Within a day, we had our best customers posting their love of Maize Quest on the site.

When Google Maps added reviews, we used a similar campaign through our email list to drive our fans to post reviews on Google. The key is to make it EASY for your customers.

In your request, post the specific link to the target site, right to your page, right to the review input if you can. Be direct in your language. For instance, "If you love Maple Lawn Farms and would like to share the love, could you take two minutes to write a 5-star review for us on Google? We'd really appreciate your help as we work with all this technology to reach new apple pickers."

Yep, ask directly for the 5-star review. If your customers don't love you that much, they won't write anything, because they won't feel like they owe you the courtesy.

CHECKLIST

Cross-Site Review

✓ List where you have a strong fan presence.

✓ Choose your target review site that needs more reviews.

✓ Plan a 1-3 part series of emails or postings with direct links to promote reviews on the target site.

✓ It takes some guts to ask for reviews, but if you are doing good work for your customers, they will be happy to help you out. Once you have these reviews, then you can share your 5-star reviews EVERYWHERE.

Guest Reviews – Use Everywhere

My wife is addicted to online reviews. I promise you that we haven't eaten, visited, vacationed, or purchased anything for my family or household that my wife has not "thoroughly vetted" through online review research.

She's not alone. Check out some statistics from a study by Forbes.com:

- o 90% of consumers read online reviews before visiting a business. (2016)

- o Online reviews have been shown to impact 67.7% of purchasing decisions. (2015)

- o 84% of people trust online reviews as much as a personal recommendation. (2016)

- o 74% of consumers say that positive reviews make them trust a local business more. (2016)

The dark side of guest reviews is when they go negative. Oh, how we berate ourselves! The outrage! The injustice of it all! We take it so personally when two people out of 3,400 visitors on the weekend complain about us publicly.

Turn that review-phobia dynamic around. Use your 5-star reviews everywhere. Overwhelm the digital and real world with love shared by your fans. Sometimes you get great feedback via email, so use those quotes as additional 5-star reviews. Don't be limited to thinking reviews are only on Google or Facebook.

The plan is simple: Take screenshots of your 5-star online reviews. Use those graphics everywhere.

CHECKLIST

Places to Make Your 5-Star Review Work for You

- ✓ Make signs of great reviews to post in your store.

- ✓ End every email newsletter with a new, different 5-star review.

- ✓ Share pics of 5-star reviews from Facebook on your Twitter feed.

- ✓ Make a "picture rotator" on your website of 5-star reviews.

- ✓ Include a sheet of 5-star reviews with your group tour mailings.

- ✓ Include 5-star reviews with your press releases.

Sure, you are still going to have a few haters. But unless you are really screwing up your business service and products, you will likely have far more glowing reviews than negative ones.

Take control of online reviews by highlighting your positive reviews online AND offline. Make sure your customers see the social proof that you deliver a high-quality experience and products.

You already have the 5-star reviews. Use them to your advantage.

FOCUS AREA 3

CROSS MARKETING

Introduction

You know everything there is to know about your business. You know all the products, services, events, experiences, and specials. But your customers don't.

Your customers know very little about your business, and honestly, why should they? Your customers lead busy lives, and they know about your business only to the extent that they have occasional interactions with your company. Those interactions get them exactly what they thought they wanted, so why should a customer delve any deeper?

That is what this Focus Area is all about. In driving a deeper connection, selling more lines of products, additional services, and new seasonal events to your customers, you aren't going to take any chances.

These cross-marketing tactics explicitly introduce 'the rest' of your business to your customers.

The big payoff is that all these tactics leverage more out of your existing customers without requiring you to get NEW customers.

View this FREE Video on Lifetime Customer Value, as part of "The Cross-Marketing Multiplier."

www.HughMcPherson.com/MoreCustomers

Seasonal Shift – Events

We run a seasonal business at Maple Lawn Farms. Each fruit we grow creates its mini-season throughout the summer or fall. Fall Harvest time brings the corn maze, pumpkin patch, and apple picking, making it by far the most significant season of the year.

Because it is the busiest season of the year, we know that we have some customers who are "Apples Only" or "Corn Maze Only." Perhaps you have customers who are "Summer Produce Only," "Christmas Tree Only," "Beach Season Only," or "Strawberry Only."

The common assumption is that all the customers know about all our events. Since they know about all our products/seasons/events, they must not be interested in them which is why they don't come/attend/buy.

False. Some portion of the non-attendees are not interested, but the behavior is never universal in any group of customers. That means some of your customers simply don't attend or buy your other products because they don't know about them or haven't yet been convinced to buy.

In the past few years, we have launched a winery, started a Sunflower Festival in August, added a "Wine Your Way Out" tasting event to the corn maze in September, and begun a Holiday Pie Tasting Event in November. We are planning a full wine festival for fruit tree blossom time in May.

Each event is designed to shift a season, or market value-added products, using our existing production and infrastructure. Each event is marketed internally to our current customers, who are more likely to convert into ticket purchases and product sales because they already know and love us.

As you look at shifting your seasons using events, plan specific promotions to launch new products. Plan events in slower periods to boost lagging seasons.

Plan also to start small. Our sunflower festival was only a modest success our first year, then grew to a $100,000 event in year two when we had the worst Fall Harvest weather in 16 years.

So many other farms were interested in this season-shifting event, that we started a Sunflower Festival Mastermind group. In that group, we worked together to learn, share, and troubleshoot each farm's Sunflower event in real-time as the season progressed and the event dates approached.

CHECKLIST

Seasonal Shift – Events

✔ What is your busiest season?

✔ In which slower season do you have something to offer?

✔ How can you utilize your existing infrastructure?

✔ How can you start small to test a new event?

If you'd like to learn more about our Sunflower Festival Mastermind Program, watch this FREE presentation at:

www.HughMcPherson.com/MoreCustomers

IFTTT

One of the least expensive and easiest cross-promotions to implement is an "If This, Then That" or IFTTT promotion. It essentially becomes an automatic promotion that is activated when a customer takes a particular action.

"If This, Then That" Promo Examples:

- o IF guest purchases (2) bottles of Peach Wine, THEN guest receives $5.00 OFF Peach Picking coupon

- o IF guest purchases (2) fruit pies, THEN guest receives 25% OFF Jams & Jellies coupon

- o IF guest picks (2+) baskets of apples, THEN guest receives FREE Wine Tasting for Two coupon

IFTTT is best used to move guests into different sectors of your business. Note that in the examples above, wine customers were sent to the orchards, bakery customers were sent to try jams, and peach pickers got a FREE wine tasting. Each IFTTT promotion introduced a non-competitive activity.

The IFTTT promotions can be deployed at your cash register using an organizer with a bundle of note cards, each printed with the special offer. Simple signs at each of the cross-promoted products in your market notify the customers to the particular deal. At your farmer's market stand, place the cross-promoted items directly adjacent to each other with a sign pointing to each explaining the deal.

CHECKLIST

IFTTT

- ✓ Choose the lead item, likely a signature product that sells well.

- ✓ Choose the new, or lesser purchased item you wish to promote.

- ✓ Set the parameters of the deal so that the deal is profitable each time and increases the average sale ticket.

- ✓ Train your staff to understand, promote the offer, and know how to redeem the deal.

- ✓ Deploy the deal in your store, snack bar, or market.

Move to Complementary Product

Similar to IFTTT, moving customers to a complementary product breaks the buying pattern. In our market, the initial offer at the fudge counter was "Buy a pound of fudge, receive an additional quarter pound of fudge FREE."

This promotion was straight from the fudge company who, big surprise, had a vested interest in selling us more fudge mix. The trouble was that fudge is expensive and giving the customer more of the same product was not enhancing their experience.

My buddy Tom came up with a great promotion we immediately substituted at the fudge counter, "Buy a pound of fudge, receive a small bag of kettle korn FREE."

This promotion is a classic win-win. The customer gets a salty snack to go with all that fudge, and we deliver it as kettle korn, one of the highest profit margin items in our farm market.

CHECKLIST

Move to Complementary Product

✓ Choose a signature item to encourage a higher volume sale.

✓ Choose a high-margin, complementary product that pairs well with your signature item (such as leafy greens with your signature salad dressing).

✓ Set the volume or price that makes each sale more profitable for you.

Channel Switching Email to Facebook

After customers make the initial connection with your business, you can deepen your relationship with them and encourage repeat business using Channel Switching.

Channel Switching is the process by which you connect with a customer through various marketing 'channels' as you work to progressively become entwined in the habits of your customer's life.

Channel Switching also blunts the effect of ever more powerful spam filters, Facebook algorithm changes, and geographic relocations.

Email remains the top connection point for managing your customer relationship. Getting an email address is like getting free access to your customer's attention.

But spam filters are not your marketing friend. Even if your email remains out of the Spam mailbox, Google will likely shunt your messages into the 'Promotions' folder for all your Gmail clients.

To circumvent the email filters, try Channel Switching your customer list from Email to Facebook. You are going to specifically work to get all your email list members to also 'Like' & 'Follow' you on Facebook.

CHECKLIST

Channel Switching Email to Facebook

✓ Send an email to your list with a link to your latest video or photo collection on Facebook.

✓ In the text of the email, tell customers specifically to 'Like' & 'Follow' your business on Facebook.

✓ Next, plan a seasonal photo or recipe contest. Launch the competition via email, but to enter, customers must post their picture for consideration on your Facebook page with #yourbusinessname.

✓ Announce deadlines and entry guideline via email, but keep all interaction for the contest on Facebook.

✓ Change your email newsletter signature to include a "Like & Follow us on Facebook" link in every email.

Channel Switching Facebook to Email

Facebook's enormous power and connection to over 1 billion people make it a must-use platform. In 2018, Facebook's complete control over the interactions between its users was displayed when a significant algorithm change altered the ability of businesses to reach the newsfeeds of customers.

The January 11, 2018 announcement by Mark Zuckerburg, Facebook's CEO, included this statement:

"As we roll this out, you'll see less public content like posts from businesses, brands, and media. And the public content you see more will be held to the same standard—it should encourage meaningful interactions between people."

It was a reminder that you, the business owner, own nothing with regard to your connections with customers. Nothing. Facebook can turn off your connections with the flip of a switch, and so they did.

You have to have a strategy for Channel Switching your Facebook 'Likes' into email addresses. Email addresses, once opted-in on your list, are YOURS.

CHECKLIST

Channel Switching Facebook to Email

✓ Use a contest. With your sign-up forms in your email program, you may create a contest sign-up form with a link.

✓ Post that link on Facebook posts with your offer or 'chance to win' and a picture. Make sure to pick winners and post the winners on Facebook with the link to your next contest.

✓ Create a VIP Club. Our winery's VIP club members get special pricing, exclusive access to events and more. You can only be a VIP by signing up on our website.

✓ Create a Facebook Landing Page Ad. Facebook allows you to create Facebook Landing Page Ads, which means that you will be collecting customer data legally through Facebook. You will download the opted-in customers at the end of the campaign.

Channel Switching Email to Direct Mail

Each time a customer shares more personal data, he should be moved up in value on your list. Eventually though, Spam filters might catch your email newsletters that go to even your most devoted customers.

Channel Switch your email list to direct mail by getting your customers' mailing addresses.

You could even follow Amazon's example and create a Prime-type program. Your customers get a FREE mini batch of jams or coffees four times a year when they sign-up for YourBusinessPRIME.

You can choose to charge (Amazon does!) or not charge for YourBusinessPRIME, but you will force them to give you their mailing and shipping addresses. You would be providing your best customers samples and ordering options four times per year.

CHECKLIST

Channel Switching Email to Direct Mail

✓ Create one of your first emails in your Welcome Sequence to ask the customer to click the link and provide their mailing address for exclusive events and sneak peek product launches sent only by postcard.

✓ Create a VIP club sign-up and require the mailing address during sign-up.

✓ Create a YourBusinessPRIME program with samples sent only to your best customers who have given you their full addresses.

Channel Switching Direct Mail to Email

If you have been in business for a long time, you might have an old mailing list with plenty of names and addresses. Hopefully, you still mail to that list on a regular basis, but due to the high cost of postage, mailing is likely infrequent.

You may also purchase direct mail lists from list brokers for a particular market, such as churches or preschools. The list brokers aren't allowed to sell you the email addresses of the prospects, but routinely the broker will offer an upcharge to send an email on your behalf. (We do not recommend you use that service as the cost vs. benefit ratio is poor.)

Moving your customers from a direct mail list, in-house, or purchased list, requires the mailing piece to promote a single action. The action must have a benefit or reward for the recipient.

To get the benefit, the recipient is directed online to sign up to receive the information – a planning guide, Mamma's Secret Recipe, a coupon, or insider information. The sign-up form moves the recipient of the direct mail piece onto your email list.

CHECKLIST

Channel Switching Direct Mail to Email

✓ Review your in-house list or purchase a new list.

✓ Create the information or offer to entice online sign-up.

✓ Create an online sign-up form.

✓ Create the direct mail postcard, letter, or flyer. Include the link to the sign-up form.

✓ Mail to the list and measure the response results by the list growth.

Groupon & Deal Sites Done RIGHT

Most business owners have a Love/Hate or Hate/Hate relationship with Groupon. It's easy to understand why, as Groupon works best for certain kinds of products, services, and businesses.

Groupon's unique selling proposition has been this: To break a customer's habit of shopping, eating, attending, or utilizing the same businesses, Groupon would offer on behalf of merchants an extreme discount, similar to the Extreme Bounce Back Coupon idea.

The balance of this extreme discount would come from Groupon in the form of tens of thousands of Groupon subscribers. This enormous audience was available from and listening to Groupon. Businesses couldn't reach these people without Groupon.

Unlike print, TV, or radio advertising, Groupon's other significant benefit was that it was FREE to the merchant and Groupon only got paid a commission if the deal sold.

Sounds great, right? A FREE advertisement you only have to pay for if it sells! The burn to businesses came from the cost side. For instance, "A profitable restaurant typically generates a 28%-35% food cost. Coupled with labor costs, these expenses consume 50%-75% of total sales," says Ron Gorodesky and Kate Lange from Restaurantreport.com

If you are discounting a meal by 50% before Groupon gets its cut, you are already unprofitable on the sale. (Hope they order drinks!)

The key to working with Groupon or any deal site is to set up the discount on the "Soft Costs," then drive traffic to a "Profit Center."

In our corn maze business, admission is a very soft cost. Welcoming a guest, unlike preparing a meal, adds almost no incremental cost. Admission is very 'soft.'

Included with our Groupon deal is a "FREE Apple Cider Donut & 5oz Cider Cup." The cider and donut are very low-cost items, and to receive the treat, you must go into our farm market and bakery. The cider and donut drive traffic to the Profit Center, our bakery.

Think total Lifetime Customer Value. Groupon generates customer traffic, and we give up a lot of admission revenue for that traffic. But once that traffic is on our farm, everything else those customers purchase, such as drinks, meals, pumpkins, and gem mining, is full price.

Groupon and deal sites aren't for every business, but done correctly, you gain access to the captive audience Groupon alone controls for ZERO cash upfront.

CHECKLIST

Groupon and Deal Sites Done RIGHT

✓ Choose your 'Soft Cost' to discount.

✓ Choose your 'Profit Center' to which you will drive traffic.

✓ Use a spreadsheet to calculate the promotional value, subtract the discount, and multiply by your percentage retained.

✓ Determine if deal sites are a fit for you.

Big Spender Tracking

Everybody likes to feel special, especially when they are paying for it. The same holds in your business. The RJMetrics in a loyal customer study found that "loyal top 10% spend 3x more per order than the lower 90%, and your top 1% of customers spend 5x more than the lower 99%."[5]

The meaning is clear: You need to track and reward big spenders. We've covered using your POS to spot the Big Spenders, but once identified, you need a plan to keep them engaged and keep them buying.

---

[5] https://rjmetrics.com/resources/reports/ecommerce-buyer-behavior/

CHECKLIST

Big Spender Tracking

✔ Brainstorm a new name for your "Big Spenders," preferably one that sounds complimentary and does not remind them of how much they spend with your business.

✔ Review your POS to identify where you get the Big Spender List.

✔ Export the list of Big Spenders to your Email list as a segment, a list you can send to without e-mailing everyone else.

✔ Ensure you have the Big Spenders' mailing addresses. If not, review "Channel Switching Email to Direct Mail."

✔ Plan your first Big Spender exclusive event and RESIST the temptation to open the event to everyone else. It must be exclusive.

✔ Plan a quarterly gift, event, surprise, mailing, or a box of samples that you will send to the Big Spender list. Remember: They are worth it!

FOCUS AREA 4

ONLINE TICKETING

The instant your customer decides to make a purchase, your system must be ready to take the order. In this section, I'll be using "online ticketing" and "online store" interchangeably as examples. The key is that your online presence allows you a direct connection with your marketing program.

Online ticketing is a valuable tool in your sales and marketing arsenal because you can direct customers straight from marketing to transaction.

Online stores allow you to track the effectiveness of online marketing campaigns through code and pixels that show the purchases attributed to each particular advertisement or email.

The new dimension in marketing is using influencers to co-promote your brand or drive traffic to your store. Only through online ticketing and tracking can you determine if you are getting value from these online influencers.

If you are not already using online ticketing or an online store for products, or an online system for booking groups or setting appointments for your business, review this section and give upgrading your online presence to allow transactions serious thought.

Online Ticketing – Instant Sale

If you run an event-based or admission-based entertainment, online ticketing creates opportunities to better plan for attendance, create scarcity with limited availability, connect directly to online marketing campaigns, and ensure customers show up, even in questionable weather.

The basic premise is that the online ticketing allows an instant sale. The moment a customer decides to visit your business, that customer can purchase tickets and cement that decision for her family.

Online ticketing can also provide crowd estimation to enable better planning. However, that did not pan out for our corn maze and fun park. We sell tickets online that can be used any day of the season, so if it rains, the ticket is still good for the next weekend. Because of that, we found customers would purchase tickets right before they arrived, sometimes the day before, but not weeks before.

For our festivals, we found online ticketing was the only way to manage the events. We created day and arrival time-delimited tickets so that a purchase committed you to a specific day and time. There were very limited days and times, only two weekends, so the event was 99% pre-sold through online tickets. We knew precisely how to staff each day for success.

SOLD OUT. Scarcity, real, or perceived is one of the benefits of online ticketing. Our first sunflower festival 'sold out' six times, because we were nervous about having enough flowers for the crowds, so we cut off tickets. Cutting off tickets and 'selling out' drove ticket sales crazy when we released more tickets because customers knew the tickets were scarce.

Using Google and Facebook advertising platforms allows you to install a Google tracking code and a Facebook Pixel on the 'Thank You' page of your ticketing or store platform. A customer can only reach that page if he makes a purchase. That means that your online advertising is tracked from the customer clicking all the way through an actual purchase. It is now possible to truly know if your ad dollars are working.

CHECKLIST

Online Ticketing/Online Store

✓ Research ticketing providers. We use TicketSpice.com, but have also used Ticketbud.com, Eventbrite.com, Ticketleap.com, Tickettailor.com, and Event Espresso, a WordPress Plugin. Each has pros and cons. Do your research.

✓ If you are selling products online, research online store options. Unless you require a customized solution, Shopify.com, Woocommerce.com, and BigCommerce.com are ready-made solutions to get your store up fast. We used Shopify.com and had our store up selling wine within 8-10 focused hours.

✓ Connect your Facebook marketing to your ticketing system using the Facebook Pixel.

✓ Connect your Google Ads account using the Google Analytics tracking code or Cname records.

✓ Online stores and ticketing are tools that reduce the friction between customer and business. Make it as easy as possible for people to buy your products and get their tickets. By doing so, you make it more likely that they will.

Need an online ticketing service? Friends of Maize Quest get a special, negotiated, 'White Glove' set-up

package when they sign-up for TicketSpice ticketing. Go to
www.HughMcPherson.com/MoreCustomers

Online Ticketing – Promo Codes

Online ticketing and online shopping cart systems offer Promo Codes to allow discounts limited to customers possessing a specific string of letters and numbers.

For instance, an offer might be formatted so that customers get "FREE Shipping with the Promo Code FREE18" added on the checkout screen.

The value for your business is that you can limit discounts to specific customers, media outlets, marketing campaigns, mailers, email lists or more to reward great customers, encourage list sign-up, or track marketing efforts by media or campaign.

Some examples:

Winery VIP customer receives the code "VIP3" for 15%OFF bottles in the tasting room.

CSA customers receive the code: "BAKETREAT2" for two monster cookies for signing up for the CSA box early.

Fall Harvest customers who have shared mailing addresses receive an exclusive "Buy ONE, Get ONE Strawberry Tart" with promo code "TART2" when they pre-purchase tickets to the Strawberry Festival.

WXCY Radio station ads promote "Buy Tickets online and save with promo code ILOVECOUNTRY"...

Each promo code operates directly through your online ticketing system, follow your ticketing or POS system Help Videos for set-up.

While you could have your web person do this, it is best if you understand how to make simple codes for basic offers. You may deploy these offers quickly through social media and email, so they should be in your skill set.

CHECKLIST

Online Ticketing – Promo Codes

✓ Confirm that your POS or online ticketing software has Promo Code functionality.

✓ Set up a simple offer code and test as though you are a customer.

✓ Plan your strategy for promo codes by media, campaign, or customers to reward.

✓ Create the promo codes for each planned event or product.

✓ Create the marketing to direct customers to use promo codes.

✓ Review and track results through your POS or online ticketing system.

Online ticketing – Employee codes

Your employees likely want to work more because they will earn more money. The best way to grow the employee hours needed in your business is to get busier.

Often overlooked, employees can be excellent promoters of your business. If you never ask them to promote the business, however, they likely will not do it on their own.

Turn your employees, not just into promoters of your business, but into rewarded salespeople. The average Facebook User has 338 friends*, plus Instagram followers, YouTube subscribers, and SnapChat friends.

Facebook friend counts

Median # of friends by age

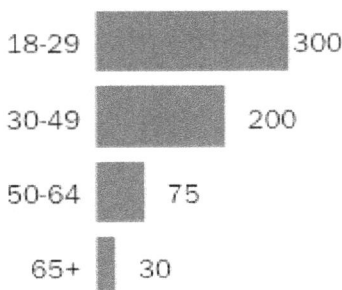

Age	Median # of friends
18-29	300
30-49	200
50-64	75
65+	30

Pew Research Center's Internet Project survey, August 7-September 16, 2013.

PEW RESEARCH CENTER

Doing some simple math, with a crew of 25 people on your roster, you could be sitting on a Marketing Channel with over 10,000 connections. If you employ 100 people, your internal marketing network could reach nearly 50,000 connections.

...and you are doing NOTHING with it.

Imagine putting some of that network to work by providing Promo Codes, exclusive to your employees, then rewarding the top Promo-Code-Promoting Employees.

It costs you nothing until after the sale is made, creates another reward stream for your best, most engaged people, and provides hundreds or thousands of social media connection points to your business.

CHECKLIST

Online Ticketing – Employee Codes

✓ Plan your program of rewards for your business.

✓ Plan the promo code terminology to make it easy to track "ER[INSERT EMPLOYEE NUMBER]" for instance.

✓ Plan your distribution system to get codes in the hands of the employees.

✓ Plan how you want employees to share or create content. This step takes EXPERIMENTATION! We do not allow our employees to have cell phones on customer-facing shifts, so when will you allow employees to create content? Are they only allowed to share content you create? Can they create content that YOU then share?

✓ Hold an employee meeting describing why, how, and the rewards for participating.

✓ Track the codes weekly or monthly, whichever makes sense for your business.

✓ Plan the public appreciation for top sharers, and end of season rewards as well as weekly rewards to keep the team motivated to share all season long.

Online Ticketing – Influencer Codes

Influencer Marketing is a new field of promotions based on promoting your business or products through the collected audience of a Social Media Influencer.

For example, if Rachel Ray tweets about your incredible apple pie preserves right before Christmas, your online store is about to crash because she has 4.44 million followers.

It used to be that "you couldn't buy that kind of press," but now you can. Working with influencers is a tricky business, however. Follower numbers can be inflated. For local businesses, you may only be within driving distance of a small fraction of an influencer's audience.

The answer is to track response to influencers using promo codes. When you work with an influencer, such as a Mommy Blogger near your farm, give her an exclusive Promo Code to include in promotions. You offer her audience a special deal, and in return get valuable tracking data to see if the promotion was successful.

Influencer marketing is in its infancy. In the past, we have offered free event tickets, free activities for moms and kids, even VIP passes, and have not had to pay the influencer. The ONE influencer we did pay, we tracked the promo code use, and it wasn't effective.

CHECKLIST

Online Ticketing – Influencer Codes

✓ Seek out influencers that 'fit' your business, products, or events.

✓ Connect to create a working relationship.

✓ See if their advertised rates fit your budget, but propose to trade value FIRST.

✓ Create a separate code and offer for each influencer.

✓ Track results of each influencer.

FOCUS AREA 5

OTHER PEOPLE'S PEOPLE

You don't know enough people. Luckily, you might know people who know more people. Their people plus your people might be enough people to move the needle on your business.

Working with other people's people is a process. You have to find people with people. Create an idea that benefits you, the other person or business, AND their people. That creative process takes time and energy which is precisely why most business owners don't do it.

You need a win-win-win. A win for your business is accessing new customers you do not typically reach and convincing them to attend, eat, or purchase.

A win for the other person or business owner might be a great deal for their followers, a special bonus for their customers, or reciprocal access to your people.

A win for the person's people is exclusive access, limited edition products, or a discount or bonus for purchasing.

In constructing a win-win-win campaign, keep in mind that you are responsible for all angles of the deal. You must take full ownership of getting everything done, such as making the brochures, formatting the emails, following up with each party on the timeline, creating the posts, etc.

It's nice to think that your collaborating 'partners' will work together on the project for their own best interest, but in reality, if you want it to happen, you better take full responsibility.

The Sacred Trust. If you are entrusted with other people's people, be it in the form of an email list, mailing list, or face-to-face connections at the partner locations, you must uphold the sacred trust. The Influencer, Event Partner, Marketing Partner, or Venue is entrusting their hard-earned customers to you and your care.

If you violate that trust by spamming, connecting outside the partnership, or just generally providing low-quality products, services, or customer interactions, you have burned a bridge you can never rebuild.

Think about it. Imagine you allowed a wine vendor into your market to do tastings. Maybe the winery even paid you $500 to get a spot during your busy Christmas season.

During their allotted tasting run after you emailed your customers that XYZ winery would be there Friday & Saturday 12PM-5PM, the winery employees showed up late, poured tiny tastings, argued with customers, and left their tasting bar a sticky mess for your customers to lean against.

Was it worth $500? Would you EVER let them come back? Do your customers think more or less of you?

Using other people's people can be an effective, efficient way to reach new customers. You must thoughtfully plan your program, execute all sides of the plan, and treat your relationship with end customers with a sacred trust.

Other People's People – Influencer Marketing

Does influencer marketing matter?

According to Nielsen ratings, the NFL Sunday Night Football program ended the season with an average of 18.285 million viewers.

You would need almost twice that – 32 million subscribers – to reach YouTube's Top Ten rankings. The number one spot is poised to change from "PewDeePie" at approximately 66 million to "T-Series" channel topping 70 million subscribers.

The crazy part is that YouTube channels can post content for viewers any time they want. They are not limited to once per week like most TV shows.

Influencer Marketing is reaching out to the audience amassed by a YouTube channel, celebrity, organization, or personality with your product, service, or event.

A few tips on working with influencers:

- Shoot for the stars, but work with the locals. If you are a local business, search for influencers locally first and gain some experience. It might be great to have Rhianna tweet about your apple pies, but it might use up a lot of your time chasing her down for a tasting. Find local foodie bloggers first.

- Start with trades, not cash. If you plan to work with Mommy Bloggers in your area, offer them a free day at your event, 10 tickets to offer their readers as prizes, a meet the winemaker party for six, or other products or services that make sense for your business.

- Spend time researching. Just because a local Instagram starlet has a big audience, does not mean it makes sense to partner with her. If her feed focuses on extreme fitness and travel, that might not mesh with your Feed the Homeless non-profit. Know what fits before you approach to save your time.

- Loosen the reins. Many Influencer brands were built by a person who "does things his or her own way." You will NOT be able to script influencers as you script your TV commercials. You'll have to hand over the products or give the tickets to the event and let whatever happens, happen. If you are not comfortable with that, don't use influencer marketing.

You are valuable to them, too. Many businesses have extensive social media, email, and customer lists. Maize Quest Fun Park, Maple Lawn Farms, Sunflower Festival, and Maple Lawn Winery combine for over 42,000 Facebook followers. That could be MORE THAN some local influencers, but their followers might not have heard about us, yet. Be confident that YOU have something to offer THEM, too.

Influencer marketing examples:

1. You connect with a guy who creates a brewery video series on YouTube to visit your brewery for the launch of your new signature Jalapeno Lager.

2. A fashion and makeup blogger girl with killer Instagram posts could be your best bet for marketing your Sunflower Festival.

3. Local Chef turned minor celebrity connection has you bringing the freshest ingredients from your CSA in weekly for a "Farmer Challenges the Chef" segment on the restaurant's YouTube channel.

4. Mommy blogger offers a "Mommy & Me Meet-up" – an in-person event at your pumpkin patch on a Thursday – with exclusive admission deals and access for her blog readers.

CHECKLIST

Other People's People
– Influencer Marketing

✓ Research local influencers that make a sensible connection to your business and products.

✓ Collect your social media stats, email lists, Facebook fans, and video views to provide cross-marketing to the influencer.

✓ Plan first what you will offer in place of cash, including cross-marketing the influencer to your business' platform of followers.

✓ Reach out via the influencer's preferred social media or via his/her contact page.

✓ Build a relationship to explore ideas for working together.

✓ Share your ability to promote THEM to your customers in trade.

✓ Determine if the offer of free products/services/tickets, trade services, or cash payments makes sense for the influencer's marketing reach.

✓ Make a marketing calendar of how many posts, videos, pictures, and links you each will provide for the other.

✓ Write out the details of the deal, before you begin any promotion.

Other Peoples' People – Marketing Partners Online

Online, every connection is a connection. In the olden days when newspapers were the central media outlets, a business would get an event or a product launch listed by contacting the press and convincing the "What's Happening" editor to insert a listing.

The traditional media outlets now look online to find out what's happening before sending reporters out to cover the news. We found this out because our Facebook Event listing brought us TV coverage from our local Fox affiliate.

Marketing Partners Online is a name for your plan to find partner sites on which you may list your events or join a list of restaurants, vendors, or service providers.

Often these partners are free, or some form of marketing is included with your membership.

Marketing Partners Online might include:

- o Local Chamber of Commerce
- o Local Visitors Bureau
- o Local Newspapers' online event listings
- o Farm Bureau listings
- o Trade or association membership links
- o Regional tourism programs or online maps
- o Wine Trails
- o Magazine Sites for kids and parents

The key is to make sure that the listing includes a link to your website, preferably to the right page of your site.

For instance, if you offer honey products and you get a listing from your local beekeepers' organizations, make sure the link sends viewers to your honey products page, not to your preschool tour program.

CHECKLIST

Other People's People

– Marketing Partners

✓ Review your existing memberships for listings and links.

✓ Review your local media sites for event postings or local lists of businesses like yours.

✓ Prepare the text and the link where you'd like each organization or media outlet to direct link clicks.

✓ Work to find at least ONE new Marketing Partner Online each week.

Other People's People – Event Partners

Event partners are a natural fit for local businesses.

With event partners, you are using the traffic to the event created by the event promoters to sell your products. Often, as with booth fees, there is a cost, but the event should either provide a much larger attendance than your home business or a new set of customers you do not routinely see at your other locations.

With event partners, you could be the promoter. We used our "Wine Your Way Out" wine tasting event as a tool to invite other wineries to offer tastings at our farm. We were the promoter then used their email lists and social media presence to market the event.

CHECKLIST

Other People's People
– Event Partners Ideas

✔ Get a booth at the local fair.

✔ Get a spot at the town's New Year's celebration.

✔ Put a float in the local parade.

✔ Take your wines to a wine festival off-site.

✔ Hold a wine festival at your winery and invite other wineries.

✔ Hold a cheese tasting at your dairy farm and invite 5 wineries.

✔ Donate tickets to the local Moose Club's Annual Bingo Party.

✔ Hold a Nail Tech Christmas Gel Polish competition at your hair salon.

✔ Partner your nail salon with local hairdressers, spas, makeup store, limo service, and dress rental businesses to give away Ultimate Prom Makeovers and you ALL get to share the giant list of prospective teen girls who enter for a chance to WIN three weeks before prom. The event is then filmed for YouTube as the winners go through the transformation and posted on Facebook LIVE during the treatments.

Other People's People – Co-location

No business can be all things to all people. Instead, try locating your business with another business that already has good traffic, but cannot offer your products. Complementary products are the key to good co-locations.

CHECKLIST

Co-location Ideas

✓ Farmers Markets are one of the original co-location businesses. You are a great mushroom grower, the next guy's the king of tomatoes, and the next lady grows killer strawberries. While each business has its fans, all the business customers shop the market for variety and efficiency.

✓ Our local grocery store offers six feet of counter space to a sushi maker. The sushi guy saves on rent, and the grocery store sells real, delicious sushi.

✓ Hillshire Farms only recently started opening stores. Hillshire built its summer sausage and cheese gift basket business by co-locating in shopping malls during the Christmas Season ONLY.

- ✓ I have a farm market client who leases space to a winery in his market because his customers wanted wine but he doesn't make it.

- ✓ My local car dealership service center has an Enterprise Rental Counter inside the dealership because that's where you'd need to rent a car!

- ✓ In governmental services, co-location is often seen when Child Services, Welfare, Housing Assistance, Job Training, and Counseling services are all located in the same building.

FOCUS AREA 6

SOCIAL MEDIA ADVERTISING

Social media is everywhere, and, in some form, connected to everyone. As social media becomes ubiquitous in connections, no single person could consume all the posts from all her friends throughout a day.

This avalanche of postings is being filtered. Facebook – our focus for this book – devises, changes, and applies an algorithm (a formula) to determine which posts you see in your newsfeed.

This algorithm is uncrackable and top secret which means that anyone telling you they can teach you to 'hack the algorithm' is lying.

The trend is evident: In a crowded field, with limited space available in newsfeeds, the days of Free Advertising through posts to all your subscribers is over.

You still must post on a regular basis to your Facebook page. Some people will see those posts, some of the time for FREE! However, if you want people to look at your posts reliably, you are going to have to pay for it.

When we discussed building your in-house customer list, we mentioned that you do not own your Facebook Fans. As evidenced by the algorithmic changes recently, Facebook is in complete control of the access to fans of your page. You do not have any choice in the matter other than to work as hard as you can to pull your Facebook Fans from Facebook onto your in-house email or direct mail list.

In our course, "Social Advertising: DECODED" we go into depth and walk through each step of the following advertising and marketing tactics. Each tactic is available to you as part of Facebook's Business Manager, an enhanced management tool provided free from Facebook through your Facebook page. To register, visit:

http://business.facebook.com.Multiplier

Get our full course at
www.HughMcPherson.com/MoreCustomers

Social Advertising – Lead Ads to Capture

Facebook and Google ad platforms started to drive traffic to web pages by creating a link for customers to click. Google would count that link click and charge you, the advertiser. You would receive the 'traffic' or the 'eyeballs' of the potential customers.

Web page traffic can be hard to quantify in terms of value. Sure, Google sent you a bunch of clicks, but did that traffic turn into sales? Previously, unknown.

The good news? You can now track clicks to sales using Facebook's Pixel or Google Analytics. If you install a little piece of code on the 'Thank You Page' of your online store or ticketing software, online advertisers can track a prospect from click to purchase.

That's OK for immediate online sales. In your business, there are likely some longer-term sales cycles for products, events, or services that will not be impulse-purchased online though, such as an event in the distant future or a large school tour that requires approval, or a Christmas tree that must be chosen and cut in-person.

You need to advertise now to capture leads to follow up with and market to over time. That is what Lead Ads are designed to do. You are going to pay to gather customer data to build your in-house list.

Lead Ads become a primary source for building your list, as we learned in Focus Area 1: Grow Your Customer List. They work best if you connect them to an automated system, such as MailChimp,

Infusionsoft, or Constant Contact as discussed in Focus Area 2 CRM: Marketing Using Your Customer List.

For a prospect to give you her name and email address, you must offer something in return. That special something is called a Lead Magnet. It could be a secret recipe, a guide to scheduling a great preschool tour, a special offer, or a Top 10 Apple Storage Tips. It must be real, high-quality information. It must have perceived value to your prospects. It must be a fair exchange.

CHECKLIST

Social Advertising – Lead Ads to Capture

- ✓ Choose your target audience – men who love farm equipment, women with children under 5, fruitarians, organic farmers, market shoppers, etc.

- ✓ Create the lead magnet for your target audience and make it valuable!

- ✓ In Facebook or Google, start by creating a campaign to "Collect Leads." Follow the instructions to connect your CRM, such as MailChimp.

- ✓ In your CRM, write a series of emails following up on the requested Lead Magnet, similar to the Welcome Sequence you wrote in Focus Area 1: Welcome Sequence – Offers & Introductions

- ✓ Run the ads with a $100 budget and see the results by viewing how many NEW customers you added to your customer list.

- ✓ Check in your CRM for results of customers clicking your email links to other services or products.

In our course, "Social Advertising: DECODED" we go into depth and walk through each step of the "Lead Ads to Capture" advertising and marketing tactics. Each tactic is available to you as part of Facebook's Business Manager, an enhanced management tool provided free from Facebook through your Facebook page. To register, visit:

http://business.facebook.com

Use Code: BK30 to SAVE 30% on our full course at www.HughMcPherson.com/MoreCustomers

Social Advertising – Event Ads

Facebook Events are a category separate from regular posts or using Facebook LIVE video. The unique FB Event features allow you to generate a community around a specific event, list dates and times, and keep comments and posts about the event from getting lost in your page's general feed.

Facebook Events are also searchable in the Facebook Mobile app. Your customers receive notifications when their friends are liking or attending local events. We discovered that new reporters from traditional media search local events for news story ideas! We booked a TV station because they searched for local events and found our Sunflower Festival listed on Facebook.

Promoting events is a different process from Lead Ads, Conversion Ads, or FB Offers. The goal of event ads is to get event responses from potential customers, typically either "Interested" or "Going."

By garnering more Event Responses, your event gets real people connected to your business. Facebook shows all your future updates to event respondents at a higher rate. Facebook notifies friends of respondents that their friends have connected to your event.

CHECKLIST

Social Advertising – Event Ads

✓ Create a Facebook Event starting at your business Facebook Page.

✓ Create a customer Facebook Event Banner using a formatting tool such as Canva.com to ensure an excellent looking event listing.

✓ Complete all the details including descriptions, ticketing links, pictures, and event banner.

✓ Click the share button in the event listing to share the event to your business page at least once per week leading up to the event.

✓ Share the event to your personal profile, and encourage your staff to do so as well.

✓ In the Facebook Ads Manager, create a New Campaign, choose "Engagement," scroll down and choose 'Event Responses."

✓ Complete the Facebook Ad Campaign and launch.

Social Advertising – Conversions

Tracking advertising to conversions is the Holy Grail for marketers. For an e-commerce business, this process can be seamless. A customer sees your ad online or on Facebook, clicks the ad, goes to your website, places an order for your exclusive widget, completes the transaction, then the Thank You page code or pixel 'fires' and you see the number of sales made vs. the spend on advertising in a dashboard on your computer.

Sounds great! However, I'll share with you that with local businesses, farm markets, and corn mazes or festival events, tracking sales by conversions is a little trickier because of friction in the 'real world.'

The set-up. To track advertising to conversions, you must install the tracking code (Google) or tracking pixel (Facebook). Typically, you place this code in the header of your web page or on the 'Thank You' page of your online ticketing system. This code sends the message of "Sale Made!" to the marketing platform such as Facebook.

The tricky, real-world part of this is that, yes, you could spend the rest of your natural life setting up online product tracking to know precisely which ad led to which product purchase, but the time it would take is unwarranted.

Save yourself A LOT of time and use tracking by conversions to give you the trend, direction, or momentum of your marketing efforts.

For instance, we track conversions in our online ticketing system. That system offers 4-6 combos, all at different prices, and I'll never know if they bought 1, 2, 4, or 9 tickets – and it DOESN'T MATTER.

Our choice was to assign a value of $48 (four tickets at $12 each) as the conversion value. We understand that '$48' doesn't capture all the details, but it will indicate the sales direction and response. Any time a customer triggers the 'Thank You' page tracking Pixel after viewing an ad, Facebook's marketing platform indicates a purchase of $48.

That's good enough to see if a campaign is working. If you sell gift baskets and the average basket is worth $75, set conversions at $75. If you sell online classes and the class costs $197, set conversions for that.

The big win is to make sure that you have a system in place to take an order, sell a ticket, buy a gift basket, and take advantage of a customer who is ready to BUY. Once you have some campaigns working, use the data to dial in which ads and audiences work best.

CHECKLIST

Social Advertising – Conversions

✓ Install the tracking code or pixel on your website as directed by your ad platform.

✓ Choose your reasonable conversion value for the items you are selling.

✓ Install the conversion code or pixel with the value assigned on your 'Thank You' page.

✓ Build your ad campaigns based on tracking conversions, not 'clicks' or 'traffic.' In Facebook, choose 'New Campaign,' choose 'Conversions,' and select your Facebook Pixel during Ad Creation.

In our course, "ViewsToVisitors" we go Click-By-Click so you get a streamlined, inexpensive, straightforward action plan to set up the THREE Facebook Ads campaigns you should use for every event or product launch.

Get your first campaign up and running in an hour & use Code: BK30 to SAVE 30% on our full course at: www.HughMcPherson.com/MoreCustomers

Social Advertising – Facebook Offers & Offer Ads

Facebook Offers are coupons you give to your Facebook Fans, or ads you run to attract new customers. The offer portion of the promotion is simply a coupon. The tracking feature is what holds the value for you.

Example ad copy that adds a bit of humor and is fun to read:

Get 10% OFF our brandy-infused Apple Infusion. It's a gorgeous, slender 325mL bottle filled with apple-y goodness at 18%ABV, so plan to sit by the fire and stay home to enjoy this one. Makes a great gift for a friend you like or an in-law that you wish liked you better.

Facebook Offers are created directly from your Facebook Page news feed. Click "Offer" instead of "Create Post." Creating Offers in the newsfeed is limiting because you are at Facebook's Newsfeed filtering mercy. It's a fine option to use though, as it is free and your fans may share it.

CHECKLIST

Social Advertising
– Facebook Offers & Offer Ads

✔ Create a Facebook Offer in your business newsfeed.

✔ Create a Facebook Offer Ad from Facebook Business Manager to duplicate your newsfeed offer. Create a New Campaign, choose from "Traffic," "Conversions," or the newer "Store Visits" as your campaign objective.

✔ Choose Continue, then the next screen allows you to turn the Offer Toggle Switch "ON."

✔ Once in the offer creation screen, input the offer details that make sense for your product, service, ticket, or promotion, such as "Offer Type," "Discount Amount," "Discounted Items," "Expiration," "Online/In-Store", "Promo Code," "Description" and "Terms/Conditions."

✔ Choose your audience as you would for any other Facebook ad set. In my case, I chose "Women within 15 miles of Bel Air Maryland over 21 years old" for the example ad above.

✔ Add a picture or video for your ad.

✔ Choose "Publish," then analyze the results as data comes in.

✓ Prepare your staff to redeem offers for in-store promotions.

Timesaver Tip:

Take your time completing the offer information and make sure to Copy & Paste your text into another program, such as Microsoft Word, Grammarly, or my favorite tool Evernote, to build up a word bank of promotional language to use in future promotions without recreating every offer.

Social Advertising – Facebook LIVE Video

Facebook's ever-changing algorithm purposefully filters out your marketing messages, posts, pictures, and even videos. However, when Facebook pushes into a new media category – in this case, LIVE video – it does the opposite of filtering; Facebook will actively market your content for you.

The theory is that Facebook wants all of our attention, and people are very likely to give more attention when something is happening LIVE.

A Facebook LIVE video starts when you choose to post from your business page and select the LIVE option, which is depicted by a little red camera. Input your description text, click the "Go Live" button and you are streaming to your page instantly, LIVE on camera.

Facebook then notifies your fans that you are 'LIVE right now!' so they may click to see what you are doing. That's how LIVE Video works as a different marketing tool... once LIVE, Facebook collects an audience for you. Your LIVE Video lives on if you choose to save the post after your LIVE shoot.

In promotion of our Sunflower Festival, we used Farmer Hugh LIVE extensively with updates from planting, picking, flying over, explaining varieties, and LIVE from the festival interviewing guests.

Tips for going LIVE and engaging customers:

- Authenticity builds connection. Farmer Hugh makes mistakes, gets things wrong, trips over branches, takes wrong turns, and is generally a real person, even vulnerable. If you are worried about your crops, tell people you are and tell them why!

- Keep it uplifting. You can be real about it without being a "Debbie Downer." No one needs more bad news. They want you to entertain them.

- Make a drastic or silly move within the first 3 seconds. During your live broadcast, do something dramatic, unusual, or silly within the first 3 seconds, so that when the video is saved, and customers are scrolling their feeds later, your video will grab their attention and make them stop scrolling.

- Get the bulk of your messaging out within the first minute, then fill in details and explore fields, and do more later. After one minute, viewership drops off a cliff. Add messaging in the middle and end with a wrap-up.

- Plan your video, but do not read a script. This isn't supposed to be perfect; it's LIVE and REAL.

- Highlight the big, gorgeous, tasty, bubbling, amazing, interesting, visual parts of your business or of a process. Giant pumpkins, wine bottling, filling cider jugs, rolling pie dough, pressing blackberries, slicing pepperoni, anything behind the scenes, in the tractor, on the apple grader, pruning in the orchard – the rule is: "What you find ordinary, they find extraordinary."

- Highlight special people in your business. If you have the Donut Queen, show her doing her thing! If you have a crazy Bavarian Nut Glazer, show him in his Lederhosen! Do an in-cab ride-along in your corn planter. Do a Farm Market tour and introduce yourself and other friendly vendors.

- If you are scared to do it by yourself, recruit a funny accomplice or hand off the Facebook LIVE duties to one or two funny staff people with your list of things to feature.

CHECKLIST

Social Advertising – Facebook LIVE Videos

✓ Make a list of things to feature that are visually interesting or different on your farm.

✓ Grab your smartphone.

✓ Go LIVE and see what happens.

Focus Area 7

Turn Your Employees into Salespeople

In my first book, *The 31-Day Workforce Turnaround*, I tackle people problems head-on. If your people aren't doing what they are supposed to be doing, it's your fault; it's my fault.

The 31-Day Turnaround book and the Agritourism Business Manager Boot Camp online program work to take the pain out of employee management, to build systems and expectations to guide the daily work-life of you and your people.

But what if those employees were salespeople? What if they went beyond merely filling orders or answering the phone or checking out pumpkins or rolling pizza dough and became promoters, became salespeople?

Your employees are a vastly underutilized sales-force. They are the last people a customer sees, talks with, or asks a question of before making a purchase. What if they used that time to sell?

You are an island of one. You can only do what one person can do within the constraint of 6-8 hours in a day. You can try to work 10-18 hours in a day, but that's not a realistic expectation. Science would challenge that you aren't useful past 6-8 hours. You might be at work, but you won't be productive.

If you have 2-3 employees, that's 2-3 times the number of interactions your business has with your customers. Some of our Boot Camp graduates have 10-20 employees, some 50 or 100 or even 400! Nothing can move the needle in your business faster than each of your employees contributing to increasing sales BEYOND top-notch quality service.

As we discussed in "Focus Area 4 – Online Ticketing, Employee Codes," employees can become a source of sales referrals, but this Focus Area targets training and selling in your business when interacting with real customers face-to-face.

Employee Scripting for Sales

Your new, young, and seasonal employees simply cannot be trusted to come up with the right thing to say when a customer asks a question or puts them on the spot.

So don't trust them. Script them.

In our Boot Camp program, we like to say that, "IF you can't commit to writing down your expectations, then you aren't committed to improving."

Scripting your staff is the process of sitting down to write out your answers to the most likely questions your team will be asked, according to staff position. That means writing down what the fudge counter people are asked routinely, the tractor drivers, the checkout staff, the corn maze crew, the bakers, the field staff, the pumpkin checkout, the delivery people – EVERYONE.

Why? Because if they don't know what to say, they are going to make something up, and there's no telling what that could be.

Example from our Snack Bar Cashier Job Description:

Key scripts for an employee to use with guests:

"Hey guys, you made it out!" "How's it going, gang?" "Having fun out there?" "Great day for a cold drink, isn't it?"

"Alrighty then, looks like it's snack time!" "Set your drinks and snacks up on the counter and we'll get you going!"

"Oh, man. Those bacon cheeseburgers are my favorite!"

"Have you been down the slide yet?"

"Thanks so much, have FUN!"

Each set of employee scripts should be written down and attached near the workstation. Ours are taped down to the counter by the snack bar checkouts, for instance.

Each set of employee scripts becomes your training material. Have you ever tried training someone with no written materials? You can't remember what to train. They can't remember what you said five minutes ago. You ramble on and on, wasting your time and the trainees' time only to come back 45 minutes later and find that they don't know what they are doing.

Sound painfully familiar?

Script your employees, so they feel comfortable, and when they are comfortable, they can sell. Our fudge counter girls hand out FREE fudge samples, and say, "You know, if you like that fudge and buy a pound, you get a FREE bag of Kettle Korn..."

That simple script is notifying the customers of the opportunity to buy more from us and get a bonus. That is selling, and it's non-threatening to the fudge counter girls and the customer. The scripted phrase feels like a friendly suggestion to save money!

If you have seasonal items that change daily, weekly, or monthly, write down the information on an internal newsletter that is just for your employees. We call ours The Fall Harvest Weekly.

On a single sheet, front and back, we list the hours of our three businesses for the week, plus the prices of tickets, combos, apples, pumpkins and more. We include the procedure for handling group booking calls, the varieties of produce ripening, and offer redemption procedures for the major deals we have out for the week.

The Fall Harvest Weekly is laminated and placed at every cash register, food service line, orchard checkout, and pumpkin tractor cab so that, during downtime, the staff can read it and get up to speed or refer to it when guests ask them questions.

CHECKLIST

Social Advertising

✓ Write down the critical scripts for each workstation at which your staff interacts with customers.

✓ Print out, laminate, and attach the scripts to the workstation.

✓ Train and role-play through each script until it becomes natural for your staff to say the scripts.

✓ Review occasionally when things are slow in your store.

✓ Consider a simple internal newsletter with essential information for changing products, hours, events, or tickets.

Employee Expectations for Top-Notch Service

You might think that "Any reasonable person would know how to mop this floor," or "Any reasonable person would know that you don't turn the PTO mower too sharp in the orchard," or "Any reasonable person would know to take out the trash bag when the trash is overflowing," or "Any reasonable person would know not to say THAT when a customer finds a bad apple in her basket!"

Alas, there are no longer any reasonable people. What used to be common sense, is relatively uncommon now. The disconnect from bygone days, when everyone was within one generation of farm work, has never been more pronounced.

When kids grew up on a farm, they learned crucial lessons such as, "working until the job is done, not until quitting time," "sometimes your favorite animal dies even when you take good care of it," "if you don't put back your tools then you aren't ready in an emergency," and "you help out your neighbor because you never know when you might need help on your farm."

Those days of life skills coming pre-installed in your staff are over. That is the way of the world, and it is a new parameter in managing your business. The flip-side of the "no skills installed" trend, is that you often hire a blank slate onto which you can imprint your methods, standards, and expectations.

The lynchpin of our Manager Boot Camp program is the Employee Expectations Guide. When I had finally grown tired enough of employees not meeting my unwritten and often unspoken expectations, I took the time to write them down.

The Expectations Guide became the hub of our pre-hiring orientation, the guide for training, and the standard to which we hold our employees. If an employee meets the guidelines, our relationship from manager to employees is good, AND the relationship between the employee and the customer is good.

If an employee strays from the expectations, such as arriving late to work, we revisit the written policy with a system of verbal coaching, then written reprimand, then, on the third serious infraction, we let the employee go.

We haven't had to 'fire' anyone since 2009. When new hires sign the Expectations Guide, they are committing to follow it. If they choose not to follow it three times, they are choosing not to work with us.

If you want top-notch customer service to be the hallmark of your business, take the time to write down exactly what you expect from your people.

CHECKLIST

Employee Expectations
for Top-Notch Service

- ✓ Write down every job or position your staff must work at your business.

- ✓ Do that job yourself for a while, writing down each action or scripted phrase you use.

- ✓ Write down the pain points in managing your crew currently.

- ✓ Write down your expectations for each pain point that, if carried out, would eliminate that pain.

If this process seems daunting, that's because it is a major undertaking. Our Boot Camp program can take away the 'blank page' by providing you templates, pre-written scripts, copy & paste policies and a complete Expectations Guide to walk you through the process in eight online modules. Learn more about this program at:

Get a FREE Course Preview Webinar, then use Code: BK30 to SAVE 30% on our full course at www.HughMcPherson.com/MoreCustomers

Employee Training IS Marketing

For some reason, employee training feels like a waste of money. When you call 5, 10, 25, 50 people to clock in, run up your payroll, and be trained while there aren't any customers in the maze, store, or orchards, it just feels wasteful.

If that's how you feel about training, I assure you that you are WRONG. That training time and payroll you invest, should be categorized in your accounting software as "Marketing."

I have clients who will spend $8,000-$12,000 on billboards without batting an eye, then belly-ache over having five additional new hires on staff 'shadowing' a returning worker.

Those five extra people being trained cost about $300 (based on $10/hr x a 6hr shift), but the value of having five extra people ready to hold down five workstations when you're crazy busy the next weekend is worth thousands in happy customers' Facebook posts, Google reviews, and Instagram pictures.

Considering that the Lifetime Value of a single Customer could be $150, $425, or even $3.400+ − training pays off quickly. Untrained workers aggravate customers to leave and share their 'horrible experience' to 1,000 of their closest friends, and can quickly get expensive.

Do the math. Determine your marketing budget for next year, then determine the cost to train an average class of new hires before you get busy or before you go to a trade show or before you head to the farmers' market.

CHECKLIST

Do the Math Training

- ✓ (# of New Hires) X (Hours) X (Average Rate/hr) = Training Cost

- ✓ Training Cost / (Lifetime Value of 1 Customer[6]) = Customers to Cover Training Cost

---

[6] See Lifetime Value of a Customer in the Introduction.

FOCUS AREA 8

PRICING PROFITS

If you welcome 1,000 customers and they each spend $5, you've generated $5,000. To get to $7,000 in revenue, you'd need 400 more customers, but what if you could encourage each of your existing customers to spend just $2 more, each?

Throughout this book, the tips and tactics are designed to build your customer base. Unfortunately, the most expensive and time-consuming task in marketing is finding new customers and convincing them to give you a try.

Increasing customer spend instead focuses on the customers you already have, as we covered in-depth in Focus Area 3 – Cross Marketing.

One of the biggest challenges business owners face is getting the pricing right, and almost universally, business owners price goods, services, and events too low.

Think about the marketing effort: If you spend and market to generate one new sale by convincing a customer how great your event is, your ticket price surprisingly doesn't matter.

An event price difference between $9.00 and $12.00 certainly doesn't matter to your customer, but that pricing difference to you would become pure profit because the cost to acquire that customer stays the same.

If you pencil through the math and have 1,000 customers buy your product or ticket, you stand to generate $9,000 or $12,000. High to low, that's a difference of $3,000 – or the value of 334 FEWER customers you would have to convince to buy a ticket!

Why your prices are too low. YOU are the problem. Namely, your emotions. I have dozens of conversations each year with operators who will not raise prices because if they do, "No one will come."

It's a scarcity mindset. Those operators are fearful that customers aren't having a high enough quality experience to visit (or re-visit) your farm.

Fear of loud voices. Another common fear comes from a time when an operator was brave enough to raise prices and promptly got yelled at, screamed at, or received a bad online review from ONE nasty lady.

During that SAME DAY, over 500 other PAYING customers had a wonderful time, but that operator cannot shake the trauma of the screaming, nasty lady. So, henceforth, prices shall never rise again! Stick with the numbers. Five hundred customers vs. one nasty lady? Beat it, lady.

The illusion of a perfect, commodity market. Farmers in particular watch and study commodity markets, but every business class graduate knows the Law of Supply and Demand. If supply increases, price decreases. If a competitor lowers prices, all the business will flock to the competitor, and your company loses. Right?

The law isn't wrong per se; it's just that you aren't in a perfect market. In fact, every local business is in an imperfect market. One of the rare benefits of a fractured, frenetic social-media-soaked world is that it is IMPOSSIBLE for all the potential customers to get the same marketing message at the same time!

Potential customers cannot, and because they are over-scheduled and busy, WILL not, make logical comparisons during purchasing decisions. Much more important is what Danial Kahneman in his book *Thinking Fast and Slow* calls "The Availability Heuristic." Customers will make decisions based on the knowledge that is most available to them during the determination.

Therefore, unless your pricing is wildly out of alignment to shock a decisionmaker, it doesn't matter if you are priced higher than your competitors.

Example 1:

Corn Maze A: $10 per person admission

Corn Maze B: $12 per person admission

The only appreciable difference is Corn Maze B makes 20% more revenue.

Example 2:

Corn Maze A: $10 per person admission

Corn Maze B: $18 per person admission

All decisionmakers come to a full-stop and start asking why the significant pricing differential.

The customer stopping to evaluate "Why" is still NOT a bad thing. IF Corn Maze B delivers a $25-value experience for $18, Corn Maze B still wins.

However, if Corn Maze B is delivering a $12-value, Corn Maze B loses the sale and its reputation.

Does it matter if your jam is $4.75 or $5.25 to your customer? Only if you are selling the generic grape jelly, they can buy in the supermarket. But it will matter to you – to the tune of 10% more revenue per jar.

We had a client who made homemade jams from her farm's fruit. She slaved day and night to keep up as it would sell out every market day at every farmer's market stand. She'd trudge back into the kitchen to grind out another set of jam batches.

At one of our conferences, she mentioned this recurring production nightmare, and someone asked her what she was charging for a jar. "$3.00," she answered. An audible gasp from the other operators indicated to her that she was way underpriced. After talking through the fear-mindset of customer rejection, she promptly returned home and immediately raised her prices to $5.00 per jar for the following week's markets.

The result? SOLD OUT. Statistically speaking, ZERO complaints. Her jam was worth it, and so was she. She was worth a 66% raise, and you are likely due to receive a raise as well.

Pricing for profits is a crucial financial driver for your business. What if you did all the customer list-building activities in this book and when the customers started rolling in, you had carefully reviewed and appropriately raised your prices?

Look inside yourself. Look at your business, events, and products. If you are doing an excellent job for your customers, if you are providing service and experience you are proud of, then you deserve to be paid for it.

Think of the impact that brave, bold move would have on your business's success.

Pricing Profits – Charge Admission – Is your store good enough to charge admission?

If you are thinking about charging admission for the experiences you create in your business, you are following an emerging trend according to Eventbrite's Harris survey of millennials.

"Eventbrite's nationwide research of millennials (defined as Americans born 1980-1996, now ages 18-34) conducted by Harris, reveals this generation not only highly values experiences, but increasingly spends time and money on them: from concerts and social events to athletic pursuits, to cultural experiences and events of all kinds."

For fun parks, corn maze farms, family entertainment centers, and events, charging admission is standard practice. Admission is based on the experience customers receive when they enter through the gate, the attractions that are included, and even access to the opportunity to purchase more tickets to special shows, events, or activities.

Retail stores can charge admission, too. Very few charge for the right to shop in the store, but perhaps you've been to some signature stores that were such a wonderful experience, you would have paid to get in if you had to.

A better question might be, why aren't more retail stores worth an admission charge? Even if your store isn't going the admission route, you may create special events, cooking classes, knitting groups, or tastings that are admission events that take place inside your retail store, either during business hours or after.

Rules we use to guide setting an admission price:

- Extract the most money from customers in the initial transaction, then charge extra for items they'll take home or eat.

- If possible, include more and raise admission.

- Increase general admission, don't 'Nickel & Dime' customers by charging an extra $2 for every attraction.

- If an item has a long wait time or limited capacity, consider charging separately or using a combo price system.

- If an item has a high fixed cost, such as a bag of gem mining dirt, charge separately.

- If an item has a high service or staffing requirement, such as birthday parties or rock climbing walls, charge separately.

- Always charge separately for food.

Some questions for determining an admission price:

- How long will customers stay once they pay admission? Disney keeps you all day and sells you hotel rooms at night. They want you 'on property' every minute of your visit. If you have a high-adventure event, such as a zip line, the activity might last only 5 minutes from harness to zip.

- How many activities and attractions are included?

- How many tastings or samples are included?

- What other activities cost additional beyond the general admission? Gem mining, food, pumpkins, midway games, duck races, LIVE music, and wine tastings all might have an additional charge.

- What do other similar, but not directly competitive, experiences cost near you? The movies, mini-golf, fast casual restaurants, salon experiences, festivals, etc.

- List each activity, its price and approximate length of experience in a spreadsheet. Next sort by price, then by time to see where your event fits.

- How novel an experience are you creating? Novelty increases the price. Our sunflower festival, for instance, is a one-of-a-kind event that is only open for six days a year. Our local bowling alley is open seven days a week ALL year.

CHECKLIST

Pricing Profit –
Charge (or Raise) Admission

✓ Clearly define the experience your business delivers.

✓ List items, activities, experiences included in general admission.

✓ List items, activities, experiences NOT included in general admission that are available for an additional charge.

✓ Create signage to explain both lists clearly.

✓ Create website and email text to explain the admission value clearly.

✓ Train your staff to understand and explain the value in the admission price.

Got questions on pricing and admission? We have a FREE Video Series on Event Pricing & Admission for you to check out with more on the topic at:
www.HughMcPherson.com/MoreCustomers

Pricing Profits – Combo ticket pricing

The goal of using combo ticket pricing is to increase the average customer spend, and encourage upsells by creating savings when the customer purchases options as a bundle.

For example:

- The cost of admission to our fun park is $12.

- One ride on the trackless train is $7.

- The retail price of both attractions is $19.

- The combo price is $15, creating a perceived savings of $4 or approximately 20%.

Here's the big pricing secret: Most experiential activities' prices are assigned entirely at your discretion. The train ticket has a value of $7, because we set it at $7, not because there is a "universal train ticket value chart."

In fact, we set the price at $7 specifically because our real target was $15 for the customer spend! The rules still apply that the prices you choose for your retail value and your combo ticket values must fall below the point at which someone is so shocked, they decide to say 'No' or further investigate.

CHECKLIST

Pricing Profit –
Combo Ticket Pricing

✓ List the activities or experiences NOT included in general admission you could use to create combo tickets.

✓ Create retail pricing or use your existing pricing to assign "Retail Values."

✓ Create combo ticket pricing with an attractive discount to encourage a customer to purchase the combo ticket upfront.

✓ Create signs explaining the value of the combo tickets.

✓ Train your staff to suggest the combo tickets, encouraging the customer to save with a combo.

✓ Pricing Profits – FREE Shipping done RIGHT

Pricing Profits – You never have a package too big

When we opened our winery in December 2015, it was our first foray into the alcohol business. The wine business has also proven much more challenging due to inventory management and long production times.

In the Corn Maze, I could sell an additional 100 tickets, and the customers would come in and have a great time. We might not even notice an additional 100 people! Yet, in the wine business, when we sold out of our Blueberry Blossom wine, we were MONTHS from restocking because it needed to ferment, filter, clarify, and then be bottled, labeled, and prepared for sale.

In pricing, the wine business is a wild frontier. Wine is so subjective to the taste and whim of the drinker, and there is no set method for pricing. To me, that meant we could effectively set prices at whatever we wanted, and so we did.

Bottle prices opened at $12.97 for our apple and peach. Why? Because we were scared that no one would come to the tasting room! After 30 days, we raised prices to $15.97, and no one seemed to notice.

Our blueberry and cherry wines came next, and they were a pain to make, so I indignantly set the price at $18.97 a bottle for them. Our brandy-infused apple and cherry specialty dessert wines come in beautiful, slender half-bottles. Just before pricing them at $22 per bottle, we hosted a cider maker's workshop and, after a tasting, we jokingly asked the makers what they thought we should charge for a bottle of Apple Infusion. Someone in the back called out, "Thirty-five bucks!" Matt, my fellow winemaker, and I were shocked, but we went with it at $34.97.

At my next Mastermind meeting, my coach and facilitator Jon Toy asked if I had made any packages for selling multiple bottles. We hadn't, so I dutifully went about pricing out a (2) Logo Glass, (1) Four-pack of hard cider (2) Bottle package – a $44 value for $37.

The next month Jon asked, "Did anyone buy it?" Yes, we sold some. Jon said, "Make a bigger package."

Next was the VIP Package – a $70 value for $57. Sold!

"Make a bigger package," said Jon.

Then came the Charter Member Package – a $167 value for $145. Sold!

"Make a bigger package," said Jon.

I said, "I need to make more wines to include before I can!"

The point is that you have customers who are willing to spend more than you think, and if you do not provide them an avenue by which to pay, they will leave your store with money still in their pockets.

Until you NEVER sell a single unit of your "Ultimate Extraordinary Combo Package" at your top price point, you cannot have a package too large.

CHECKLIST

Pricing Profit –
No Package is Too Big

✓ List items you can combine to create a package of goods or experiences.

✓ List the retail value of that package.

✓ Choose a discount rate that creates value for your customer.

✓ List your packages on signage, create concrete examples of the product package, post and email your customers that a new package is available.

✓ Train your staff to understand the value and savings of packages.

✓ Create a low, medium, and high-value package.

✓ Create a RIDICULOUS package you are 'sure' that 'no one' would 'ever' purchase.

✓ Email me when someone does.

Pricing Profits – High-Profit End Caps

In setting up displays in a retail store, the location of the product determines sales success.

In a 2014 study by Video Mining Corporation in grocery-style stores, the End Cap displays were shown to offer product exposure to 41% of total traffic, and a purchase rate of 58% to "Engaged Shoppers," i.e., shoppers who stopped to view the display.

You might not run a grocery store, but the End Cap value principle is still valuable. In your retail store, you likely have End Caps, displays at the end of aisles or similarly prominent locations that you know customers 'must see' as they move through your retail space.

In these prominent spaces, the exposure rates and sales rates are likely similar to the grocery store study, which means you need to feature your most profitable items in the highest selling spaces.

The internal challenge is that you might not think that your high-margin items fit well in that high-visibility area. You might think kettle korn belongs near the bakery, but with a profit margin over 20-TIMES cost, kettle korn belongs on your "End Cap."

CHECKLIST

Pricing Profit –
High-Profit End Caps

- ✓ Watch camera footage of your market or retail space.

- ✓ Identify the most-viewed areas. These are your "End Caps."

- ✓ Map your retail space and plan your End Cap displays.

- ✓ Review the profit margin per item and choose 2-5 high-profit items to feature in your End Caps.

- ✓ Choose a sales period that makes sense to track for your business.

- ✓ After resetting your End Cap displays, track and compare sales of End Cap items.

- ✓ Keep winning items, continue your experiment with other items.

Pricing Profits – Signature Products

Recognition is hard to come by. If you are 'known' for something, marketing gets easier. Signature products are those you become known for – products that are your specialty.

I did not understand the value of creating signature products entirely until we decided to add Apple Cider Donuts to our bakery. Cider donuts are a signature product for many Fall Harvest farms, and they are special because instead of adding water to the dough, you use fresh apple cider. The experience is enhanced because we make them fresh each day and often guests can get them warm from the fryer.

In choosing what will become your signature product, it is essential to select a high-margin product as well. Donuts are labor intensive, but the ingredients are inexpensive.

Beyond 'another bakery product.' Our donuts moved beyond being 'another bakery product' because we marketed those donuts everywhere. We included them in deal sites, such as Groupon. We added signs to the front of the market. We offered free samples to every guest, and to the best of our ability, we made great warm donuts. We delivered on the promise of our signature product.

Apple Cider Donuts have become a quintessential part of our guests' fall harvest traditions: our signature product... without which a trip to Maple Lawn Farms would not be complete.

CHECKLIST

Pricing Profit –
Signature Products

✓ Choose a product that is uniquely your own or upon which you have added your unique twist.

✓ Make sure that product has a high margin.

✓ Plan promotions, signage, and employee training to build your signature product into every customer experience.

Pricing Profits – Make Once, Sell Many Places

In the late '90s, the early days of our corn maze and fun park, we had long lines at the snack bar. Our Coca-Cola representative introduced us to the concept that more drink outlets yield increased sales.

The extra outlets didn't cannibalize snack bar drink sales but instead boosted total drink sales. We added drinks and drink machines throughout the park, and each time, drink sales increased. We would increase our shipment, accept it one place, then refill all the coolers and machines around the park.

On a North American Farmers Direct Marketing Advanced Learning Retreat, we visited Roba's Pumpkin Farm in Scranton, PA. They had a brilliant food service program, and one of their signature products was kettle korn.

We toured the kettle korn shed where they had a big production machine and sold the product. Then as we toured the farm, I saw kettle korn displays in all the barns, in the farm market, in the exit barn, and at some of the other food outlets.

They were efficiently using a big machine and staff to make kettle korn in one location, then selling the kettle korn everywhere. Roba's had not duplicated the kettle korn infrastructure, just the displays, so you were never too far from a bag of their signature product.

CHECKLIST

Pricing Profit –
Make Once, Sell Many Places

✓ Choose a product or signature product you could sell or display in more than one location.

✓ Plan your inventory and restocking system to maintain quality.

✓ Test selling your product at multiple locations while ensuring your POS system allows you to track sales by station.

Pricing Profits – Sell with Smell

Generally speaking, you cannot turn off your nose. As Amanda White at *Psychology Today* states, "The olfactory bulb has direct connections to two brain areas that are strongly implicated in emotion and memory: the amygdala and hippocampus."

The amygdala is the 'old' part of your brain that is hardwired to react with emotion and keep your body safe in a dangerous environment. That is unlike the pre-frontal cortex, which is in charge of logic and reasoning. Smells go straight to your customer's emotions.

The good, positive emotion-generating smells, as well as the bad, negative-emotion generating smells go straight for the amygdala. Managing the atmosphere of scents around your customers can be a challenge, particularly if you are on a farm.

In 2010, *bloom*, a chain of grocery stores, advertised fresh cut steaks with a scent-enhanced billboard of a fork holding a juicy bite of meat. Commuters were treated to a peppery BBQ scent as they drove by.

Jim's Steaks and Geno's Steaks have been fighting a street war in Philadelphia on South Street for cheesesteak supremacy by pumping the exhaust fans from the grill out at street-level.

Starbucks serves food, but did you ever notice that you can only smell the coffee? That's by design.

Your retail space might need just one enhancement to utilize delicious smells you already produce, perhaps from your cider donuts or Bavarian nut production.

Taking things further might require some planning and testing to ensure that you aren't crowding the atmosphere with too many competing smells. Having a plan is the key, and planning separation between scent distribution allows your scent campaigns to work sequentially.

A more cohesive scent plan might look like this:

- At the entrance to your corn maze, guests smell kettle korn and may purchase a bag to snack on during their walk in the maze.

- As they exit the maze to other attractions and pass the snack bar, you direct the French Fryer's exhaust or grilled meat scent into their path.

- A few hundred feet away, customers pass your pretzel stand with a fresh dough-baking scent.

- As they ride past the farm market, they receive a waft of "Mom's Apple Pie."

- Upon entering the market, they pass the Bavarian nut machine's warm, cinnamon aroma.

Each scent is separated by airflow and distance. Each scent coordinates with a product for customers to purchase when activated.

CHECKLIST

Pricing Profit –
Sell with Smell

✓ Map distinct areas in your retail or entertainment space that are separated by distance and airflow.

✓ Choose high-margin products to promote with scent.

✓ Decide if you can redirect existing scent or if you need to purchase scent distribution equipment.

✓ Test ONE area and ONE scent first.

Pricing Profits – Final Impulse Items

Mints, candy, and tabloid magazines are located at the checkout lines in grocery stores because shoppers have exhausted their decision-making abilities filling their carts. In this depleted mental state, making customers buy on impulse is easy.

Offer impulse items in your retail space. Plan impulse items following the same rules you see in the grocery store. Under ten dollars, easy to grab, tasty, cute, and small enough to hold in your hand.

Tanner's Farm Market offers homemade caramel candies. We keep small kettle korn bags on holders in the checkout lanes. Think penny candies, single prepackaged cookies, Rice Krispie treats on a stick, or a single piece fruit.

The key is to make it easy and irresistible for customers to grab. Mark items with clear pricing signage. The less thinking, the better.

CHECKLIST

Pricing Profit –
Final Impulse Items

- ✓ List small retail items under $10 that have a high-profit margin.
- ✓ Prepare displays to hold items at prime retail height between waist & eye level.
- ✓ Place displays directly adjacent to checkout lanes.
- ✓ Create clear signage for impulse items.
- ✓ Test products from your list to find the best impulse items for your store.

MAKE HISTORY

You are more important than you think. In a world where people pretend they are famous on social media in an attempt to become famous in the real world, you are an authentic, genuine person. You run a real business.

You provide quality products and experiences to your customers. You run a real business that has a real history. When you talk about your history, you need to make it real.

You make history by posting clippings from your past news coverage. You make history by printing pictures of your great-grandfather on canvas and hanging them in your barns. You make history by creating a timeline of your business that your customers can see. You make history by creating a map for your customers to put a pin in their hometown when they visit.

As you choose and use these tools, keep in mind that this book is a reference guide. It is not meant to be an overwhelming list for which you have to check off each and every box. Review and choose the 'low hanging fruit' (pun intended). Get started and take action immediately on ONE idea from this book – TODAY!

The goal of this book is to fuel your creativity with ideas to grow your business. Only through business growth can you ensure that you'll be making history for years to come, and perhaps, passing on your business and all the family traditions you create each year for your customers to your next generation.

Now, page back through to your favorite idea, review the checklist, and TAKE ACTION.

That's how you'll make history.

-Hugh

This is only the beginning. Keep this book on your desk for those times when you are out of ideas and out of energy, then pick it up and grab a fresh idea you can work with. Make sure to check-in online for more, sign up for our blog posts and to connect personally at:

www.HughMcPherson.com/MoreCustomers

SAVE over $5,420.13 AND 363 Hours.

The GIANT *"Get More Customers To Your Business Book Buyer's Bonus Package"* is at:
www.HughMcPherson.com/MoreCustomers

As much as I would like to include everything possible in this book, it is IMPOSSIBLE. Plus, some people learn better from hearing, seeing videos, working in groups, or doing worksheets.

So, I'm including TONS of extras, bonuses and savings as a "Thank You" for taking the first step in growing your business using the tactics in the book.
You'll find:

- ✓ Hugh's Recommended Tools – An ever-growing list of over 27 software and hardware options to help you implement what you learn in this book (363 Hours VALUE)
- ✓ Goal Without A Plan is a Wish Workshop ($697 VALUE)
- ✓ The Cross-Marketing Multiplier Presentation ($697 VALUE)
- ✓ Event Tsunami Strategic Event Marketing Program (30% OFF)
- ✓ Views to Visitors Click-By-Click Facebook Marketing Program (30% OFF)
- ✓ Social Advertising: DECODED FREE Video Presentation on Facebook Lead Ads, plus complete online course (30% OFF)
- ✓ Agritourism Manager Boot Camp – The #1 Agritourism Employee Management System (30% OFF)
- ✓ Seasonal Manager Boot Camp – A Complete Employee Management System for ANY Seasonal Business (30% OFF)

- ✓ Platinum Set-up Package from TicketSpice.com for our clients and friends ONLY – ($700 VALUE)
- ✓ Sunflower Festival FREE 3-Video Series, PLUS Sunflower Mastermind Group Registration ($200 OFF)
- ✓ *"Your Event Pricing Is Too Low And I Can Prove It"* Profitable pricing video Presentation ($497 VALUE)
- ✓ *"Adventures In Delegating" 5-Part* Video Series to make you an effective task delegator and free up your time ($497 VALUE)

YES! We've done ALL this stuff first-hand running our farm, pick-your-own fruit orchards, corn maze, fun park, birthday party center, sunflower festival, and winery.

YES! All this is really available to you, included.

YES! You can't do everything in this book in a single day, week, month or even year.

YES! You can reference what you need and get back to work QUICKLY, so keep this book handy.

YES! We offer plenty of ways to get MORE detailed information particularly through our popular online courses.

YES! You CAN do this! This book is FULL of positive energy to power you through each SHORT, DOABLE action step.

YES! We are REAL people and you can call me at the farm at 717-382-4878 ext. 102 to discuss ANY of our programs - *Hugh*

The GIANT *"Get More Customers To Your Business Book Buyer's Bonus Package"* is at:
www.HughMcPherson.com/MoreCustomers

ABOUT THE AUTHOR

Hugh Mcpherson, Maize Quest's Maze Master, has been "losing" guests and telling "corny" jokes since 1997 on his home farm. Maize Quest's Corn Maze & Fun Park is home to the annual corn maze, and now features the annual Sunflower Festival.

The home farm, Maple Lawn Farms, welcomes guests to pick-their-own peaches, apples, pumpkins and blueberries throughout the season. In 2015, Hugh launched Maple Lawn Winery to add value to the fruit crop and welcome a new tribe of wine-loving guests.

Maize Quest, through www.MazeCatalog.com, designs corn mazes, games, and attractions for over 85 farms in the U.S., Canada, and the U.K. The Agritourism Manager Boot Camp is Maize Quest's first online course. Having developed and trained over 800 employees, this system works with everyone from Grandma to a 14 year old in his first job. Boot Camp is the #1 program for agritourism and farms with seasonal, retail employees to build a complete staff management system. Now in its third season, Sunflower Festival Mastermind Program offers operators a group learning environment, facilitated by Hugh, in which challenges and opportunities are solved together.

Hugh served for six years on the North American Farmer Direct Marketing Association's Board of Directors (NAFDMA). Hugh also serves as the choir director at Centre Presbyterian Church in New Park, PA, and plays Ultimate Frisbee in a local league. His pride and joy are his wife Janine, daughter Annie, and son Ian.

www.ingramcontent.com/pod-product-compliance
Lightning Source LLC
Chambersburg PA
CBHW060558210326
41519CB00014B/3504